Karen Pence '07

When It's Your Turn to Serve

When It's Your Turn to Serve

Experiencing God's Grace in
His Calling for Your Life

KAREN PENCE

BROADSIDE BOOKS
An Imprint of HarperCollins*Publishers*

All art courtesy of the author.

FIRST EDITION

Library of Congress Cataloging-in-Publication Data has been applied for.

ISBN 978-0-06-330398-0

23 24 25 26 27 LBC 5 4 3 2 1

CONTENTS

Contents

Introduction

Proverbs 16:24 says, "Gracious words are a honeycomb, sweet to the soul and healing to the bones."

This book is intended to be an encouragement to each reader specifically. This is not a memoir, not a book about Karen Pence, but rather a story about how God used me in a mighty way and how He gently and patiently showed me how to wear the mantle He was placing on my shoulders. The purpose is not to shine a light on my life, but rather to highlight some of the initiatives in which I was privileged to be involved, to show the journey I traveled and the investments I made.

Each of us, on our own journey, will be offered opportunities that, difficult though they may be, we can embrace, or reject for the easy road. Everyone makes their own choices, and I do not suggest any specific path for the reader. Instead I gently toss out some breadcrumbs to take you with me as I reflect on the paths I journeyed with God.

As a child, I loved to memorize poetry. My favorite poet of all time is Robert Frost. When I was in the fifth grade, Robert

Frost's daughter, Leslie, visited the school I attended. After her presentation, she gave me a copy of a collection of Robert Frost's poetry, inscribed, "For Karen . . . because you memorize poetry." I cherished that gift, and it encouraged me to continue memorizing his poems. My favorite is "The Road Not Taken."

Two roads diverged in a yellow wood,
And sorry I could not travel both
And be one traveler, long I stood
And looked down one as far as I could
To where it bent in the undergrowth;

Then took the other, as just as fair,
And having perhaps the better claim,
Because it was grassy and wanted wear;
Though as for that the passing there
Had worn them really about the same,

And both that morning equally lay
In leaves no step had trodden black.
Oh, I kept the first for another day!
Yet knowing how way leads on to way,
I doubted if I should ever come back.

I shall be telling this with a sigh
Somewhere ages and ages hence:
Two roads diverged in a wood, and I—
I took the one less traveled by,
And that has made all the difference.

I see my life as a blessing. But there have been struggles. My parents divorced when I was four. And I, myself, divorced my first husband. The life of a political wife, too, is far from glamorous or easy, however it may seem. There have been times when I, like you, just simply had to call up a girlfriend and vent. Times where I got on my knees as the song, "The Warrior Is a Child," by Twila Paris describes: "I drop my sword and cry for just a while 'cause deep inside this armor the warrior is a child."

Throughout my childhood and early adult years, as I would experience the struggles we all go through, my faith grew deeper and deeper. The Lord was the One who was constant. Through it all, I've tried to take the road less traveled and head the way that may look uncertain, especially if I feel it is where God is ultimately calling me to serve Him and others. And no matter what, He has always gotten me through and never abandoned me.

He was always there. He still is. He is the reason I was able then and now to focus on the positives in my life, the blessings, and to take risks without fear. *When It's Your Turn to Serve* is meant to guide you, the reader, toward wearing the mantle, toward accepting the challenge, toward leading where you are called, to illustrate how, on my own journey, I was blessed by letting go of the safe and secure and embracing the risky and unknown.

I learned the truth behind Psalm 19:9b–10, "The decrees of the Lord are firm, and all of them are righteous. They are more precious than gold, than much pure gold; they are sweeter than honey, than honey from the honeycomb."

When It's Your Turn to Serve

CHAPTER ONE

Bees

*Foraging honeybees have to fly around 55,000 miles to make
a pound of honey, traveling to about 2 million flowers.*

I was running barefoot and free as a kid across a large field of grass
and clover at a playground and I remember it vividly: I stepped
smack-dab on a bee. It's not the kind of experience that makes a kid
love bees, and I was no different. Like most children, I was wary of
bees, knowing how much that sting can hurt.

But in February 2013, I found myself sitting in a room full of
other spouses of governors at the National Governors Association's annual meeting. Governors and their spouses convene at
a bipartisan meeting once a year in Washington, D.C., to share
ideas, although each party also has their own separate sessions
during the four-day weekend. I looked forward to this gathering
each year while I was the first lady of Indiana. Since the tenure of

a governor is four years, discussing ideas and offering examples of what other spouses had done meant the spouses didn't have to reinvent the wheel. Once the election is over, the job of a "first spouse" begins in full force. It can be a confusing and stressful time. Everything is new. All of a sudden, you are expected to fill a role you've likely never been in before, all while getting your family adjusted to this new lifestyle. This organization comes alongside the spouses, providing advice and suggestions for maneuvering through this strange new reality. I welcomed how these experienced spouses took the newcomers under their wing, sharing the wisdom they had gleaned as they served. I had a lot to learn. Even though I had been a congressional spouse, I knew I wanted to use my time as first lady of Indiana to make a difference. But where to start?

This particular year, Ginger Beebe, the first lady of Arkansas, delivered a fascinating presentation. She gave an entire demonstration sharing how she had bees at the Arkansas Governor's Mansion. Of course, we all technically had bees buzzing around our gardens, but she had a *beehive*. This was extraordinary to me. I had heard of colony collapse disorder—when most of the worker bees in a colony desert a hive, leaving the queen behind with food and some nurse bees to care for the young ones. I had heard about how we needed to come alongside our bees because some argue they are endangered. Not being a scientist, I didn't have the authority to weigh in on this issue. I just knew I could help honeybees, even if they aren't in danger of becoming extinct. I didn't want to wade into all of the political rhetoric and debates around what was affecting the bee population, but starting a hive seemed like an obvious way that I could do something to help. But it had never occurred to me before to have a hive. It had never occurred to me that I could support bees in my neighborhood, in my state. The Indiana Governor's Residence sits on six acres, which was perfect for a beehive. I knew nothing about bees, but I knew enough to know that I could help. I've found that God has a way of placing opportunities in my path. And this was one I wanted to investigate.

Ginger's presentation was riveting. I learned how she used the hive to teach constituents in her state about bees and then gave little bottles of honey as gifts from the Governor's Mansion. Suddenly I found myself not feeling an aversion to bees, but rather a camaraderie with these creatures. My curiosity was piqued. And so began my fascination with bees.

Years later, I was standing alongside a beekeeper in Montana, watching the myriad of bees flying all around his hive, as he told me that he could distinguish which bees were the ones returning to the hive as opposed to those heading out. Intrigued, I asked him how. He explained it was because the returning bees flew low to the ground and their sacs were full of pollen. I looked closer and I could see it for myself—the little pollen sacs on their tiny legs were full of yellow pollen. As they buzzed around, I could see how they flew lower as they carried more pollen.

I thought of that conversation many times in the future, as I reflected on what experiences I would bring back to my own hive, what lessons I could share. Having ventured far and wide like the bees in the roles in which God had placed me, I wanted to take what I had learned and apply it to my own life—and help people along the way.

As Romans 12:7a and 8 says, "We have different gifts, . . . if it is to encourage, then give encouragement; if it is giving, then give generously; if it is to lead, do it diligently; if it is to show mercy, do it cheerfully."

I knew that if God placed me in a leadership role, in a role where

He wanted me to be an *encourager*, then He would give me the grace to lead, as He will you when He calls you to different times of leadership or service. The bees' work isn't easy or quick. They don't immediately see the fruits of their labor. They travel far and wide and work diligently. Like the bees' journey, mine was going to require diligence and patience and trust, and I would end up traveling quite far and wide, too.

Since then, the bees have been a constant in my life, teaching me not only about myself, but about God's creation and His plan for me. Whenever life takes an unexpected turn, I have thought about the bees and how God perfectly designed them for the task at hand, and how He has done the same for me and will help me along the way.

CHAPTER TWO

Surprises

*Honeycomb cells have many uses other than storing
honey. They are also used to store nectar, pollen,
and water, as well as a nursery for larvae.*

It was 1984. I walked out of the church with my guitar in my left hand, headed to my little Honda Civic, parked under a big tree by the side door. It had been a great service, and I loved being part of the worship team. This was my home turf, near the neighborhood where I grew up, went to college, and then lived as I taught at a private school nearby. I was reaching into my purse to grab my keys when I was approached by a guy saying he was interested in joining the guitar group. I told him he needed to talk to the man with the beard, and he stuck out his hand instead and said, "Mike Pence." I realized then that he wasn't really interested in joining the group (although he does play guitar, and he could have backed it up), but that he was interested in meeting me.

We had a nice conversation. I shared with him where I taught (he had thought I was a college student); he said he was in law school, and I told him my sister was also at the same law school. The conversation ended without him asking me for my number, so I didn't think much else about it. Interestingly, that church is right across the street from the Indiana Governor's Residence, where we would serve thirty years later.

The next week, I was babysitting my sister's kids, and their phone rang. A man's voice asked for my sister. I explained that she and her husband were out of town. "Who is this?" he asked. I told him, and he promptly hung up on me. I think I shocked him. A few minutes later Mike Pence called back after his buddy had teased him about hanging on me. I told him I had thought it was him. He had been trying to call my sister to get the scoop on me. He had approached the registrar at the law school they both attended, but the woman was reluctant to give out personal information. He explained the situation to her, that he was interested in finding out information about me from my sister. Amazingly, she agreed to give him my sister's number, then asked him to be sure to invite her to the wedding . . . and we did! During the course of our conversation, I invited him to join us for dinner and ice skating that next weekend. And that was that. We started dating.

If something needs to get done, I don't really procrastinate. Mike likes to share a story about me from that time that might give you some insight into how I operate. He was driving a very beat-up yellow Chevy Impala at the time that had a huge rust spot on the top of the trunk, around two feet by two feet. As a surprise, I borrowed his car for the day, rented a power sander for the trunk, and then spray-painted it the same yellow. The car wasn't worth enough to take it into a body shop to have it painted, but at least it looked better after I used the matching spray paint. I don't think he expected his girlfriend to power-sand and paint his car, but it did show him that I'm someone who gets things done. He was a good sport about it, too, and joked that he was knitting me a sweater. His family and friends teased him, but it didn't bother him at all. We still laugh about that car, and it was one of the first times he saw my determination.

When we met, I was teaching elementary shop class, part of the school's art curriculum. Ever since I was little, I had always wanted to be a teacher. I never really considered doing anything else. I loved the creativity of figuring out new ways to teach something, and I loved seeing kids' eyes light up the moment they grasped a difficult concept. I also loved getting close to my students and really getting to know them. My degree from Butler University was in elementary education with a teaching endorsement in elementary art, which meant I could be a classroom teacher for any grade level from kindergarten to 8, and I also could be an art teacher. I had gotten the art endorsement on a whim, thinking it would be fun, without realizing how God was preparing me even then for the future to which He was calling me—half of my teaching career would be as an art teacher. I also learned during college that I have an affinity for painting, something I had never tried before. I love it when God shows us new gifts we possess or presents us with new interests later in life.

The role of being a teacher, being responsible for my own classroom and everything that entails, helped prepare me in other ways for the roles later in my life when I would be first lady of Indiana and second lady of the United States. A teacher needs to prepare, implement a plan, and be flexible. Those qualities certainly were needed in full measure.

When I used the shop room in the evenings, I enjoyed experimenting with stained-glass projects and creating designs out of my own pieces of wood. Once, I made Mike a stained-glass cross with a heart in the center, which was a symbol that had become one of our "things." That cross hung in our kitchen for years. We had decided early on to dedicate our relationship to Jesus Christ. On one of our early dates, I had said to Mike, "You're my number one." He stopped short and looked at me and explained that he didn't want to be number one—not above the Lord . . . that he knew there would be times when he would let me down. So we decided to put Christ at the center, and the cross with a heart in the middle became very special to us: our faith was at the center of our relationship. This was a new concept for both of us. Mike shared with me that he had prayed the night before he met me that if God would bring him the "one," he would dedicate that relationship to Him. That same symbol was on our wedding invitations and was the symbol on top of our wedding cake.

When we first started dating, I remember Mike's friends questioning him a lot about whether or not I was a Christian. Their concerns really bothered me a lot; I felt judged by them. My faith has always been an important part of my life. One night I mentioned it to Mike, and he explained that they were basically asking if I had given my whole life to God. I told him I didn't know that was what God asked for. I had been taught to not bother God with the little things, that He was too busy for me. But I told Mike that if he could show me in the Bible where it said that, I was happy to give Him everything . . . I just didn't know that was what He wanted.

I was someone who had always had a deep faith; not much Bible knowledge, but a very deep faith. I always had the conviction that God was in control, and that no matter what, He wanted the best for me. I remember asking to be dropped off at my middle school, a Catholic school, to go into the sanctuary and pray before school. I even wondered if I might want to be a nun when I grew up, but I knew I wanted a family someday, so I didn't pursue that. Mike, however, had a deep biblical knowledge, and not as much faith as I did. We made a good team right from the beginning, complementing each other's weaknesses. I hadn't really listened to contemporary Christian music before I met Mike. But he introduced me to some of the popular Christian artists at the time. These Christian musicians seemed to understand me completely. Their music sent me digging deeper into God's word. And my understanding of the Bible began to grow.

Teaching elementary shop class was a lot of fun. The kids made little turtle stools, Christmas trees out of wood with painted nails as the ornaments, and other projects. They had a fine arts teacher, as well, so I taught a lot of the projects that were similar to crafts.

While I loved teaching shop to all of the first- through fifth-grade students, I missed having my own self-contained class of twenty-five students instead of more than 125 students that I only saw for forty minutes a week. Before I took the shop position, I had taught second and third grade and enjoyed having my own little group of students that I could really get to know over the course of a year. The private school where I was teaching wasn't interested in giving me my own classroom, so I applied to the public school system for a position as a classroom teacher again. That August, I was offered a position teaching second grade in a public school.

The week before school started, Mike and I decided to go out to dinner and celebrate nine months of dating. Mike asked me what

I wanted to do, and I suggested we go to dinner and then go feed the ducks on the canal in the Broad Ripple area. It was something we had enjoyed doing before. So after dinner, on August 6, Mike pulled out two big loaves of Italian bread. I tore off the end of one loaf, and out popped a ring box! Mike got down on one knee and asked me to marry him. I said, "One moment." I think that kind of threw him for a loop, but I had a good reason.

A month before, on July 9, I had decided that if I were the one proposing, I was ready to commit to getting married. I wanted there to actually be a moment where I decided I was ready to accept his proposal. I didn't want to drift into an engagement. I wanted to be very sure in my heart that I was ready to marry him. I had our symbol—the gold cross with a heart in the middle— engraved with the word *Yes*. I planned to give him that cross when he asked me. So I dug through my purse (the whole time he was wondering why I didn't immediately say yes . . .), handed him the cross, and said, "*Yes!*"

That year of teaching was very fulfilling, and I loved having a classroom again. I became such good friends with my colleagues that they actually would be right outside the delivery room when our son, Michael, was born years later and would serve on my charitable foundation board when I was first lady of Indiana. That school year, I invited each of my students to dinner at my apart-ment in groups of five. The kids would plan the meal, do the shop-ping with me, and prepare dinner. After dinner, Mike would draw cartoons of each of them to take home with them. He is quite a caricature artist and had started drawing cartoons when he was in high school.

At the time, Mike was in law school. While there, he created a weekly cartoon, *Law School Daze*, for his law school paper. Each week, he would do a cartoon featuring "Daze," a law student who strongly resembled Mike and was kind of goofy. Many of the cartoons were specific to classes or professors, but I remember one cartoon that showed Daze in court, standing at the podium presenting a case for Moot Court, the law school trial competition each year. He was starting his argument in the traditional way, "May it please the court . . ." And Daze and the entire podium were bombarded with arrows. Moot Court can be an intimidating time where law school students are presenting an argument in front of all of their peers and several professors. It is a practice courtroom experience, and they frequently have their whole presentation taken apart piece by piece. The cartoons were a way to poke fun at himself and bring a little levity to law school. At his graduation, I gave him a bound book that included every single one of the cartoons.

We got married in June 1985, nine months after he proposed. We paid for our own wedding, and our budget was limited. We had a buffet meal and wine carafes on the tables and a DJ. We really had a lot of fun. Halfway through the reception, his brothers all threw him in the pool at the venue. I was upset at first because I thought he was going to change out of his wet tuxedo. I mean, what bride wants to dance with her husband at their wedding reception in his shorts? My mom came over to me and told me not to let this ruin the day. She helped me to focus and not dwell on something that could have been a big negative. I went up to Mike and said that I didn't want him changing out of his tuxedo because it was wet. But, with a twinkle in his eye, he simply put a towel around his neck, and we kept celebrating. The next morning, we headed to the Bahamas for a week.

For our first year of marriage, we rented a little house that is no longer there, and started our lives together. The next year we purchased our first home, located about a block from where I had attended high school. It was a cute little bungalow with a covered porch and a porch swing.

While we were dating and getting to know each other, we of course had talked about how we saw our futures. I shared with him that I loved teaching, and really wanted a family. I had always wanted to be a mom. He shared with me that he had always had a dream of someday representing his hometown in Congress. He speculated it would be some time in his fifties.

As newlyweds, we decided to get connected to our community. We volunteered as leaders of a small group of teenagers going through Confirmation at our Catholic church. This was a great church that participated in local revivals with the Baptist church across the street. The Baptist church would raise a tent and have an evening of gospel singing and visiting preachers leading altar calls for those attending to come forward and give their life to Jesus Christ. Our Catholic church encouraged each of these teens to make a personal decision to ask Christ into their hearts as their Lord and Savior. We got very close to these kids, and had them all over for dinner to our home.

Our lives were pretty content. We were enjoying a very satisfying time where we each were finally settled, working at our chosen professions, enjoying lots of friends, and establishing our marriage.

In our neighborhood, Mike was precinct committeeman, and I was the vice committeewoman, which meant we went through our neighborhood getting to know our neighbors and helping them register to vote. We would work at the precinct on voting day, which was always one of my favorite days because I got to see all of our neighbors and also have as much coffee and donuts as I wanted! One afternoon, Mike decided to go with a good friend to meet with a township official to see what he recommended Mike should be doing now to prepare to run for Congress in his fifties. The official simply said, "Run now."

Well, needless to say, that was a complete surprise. But that particular year, there was no Republican yet on the ticket to run against the sitting incumbent. Mike called me at school that afternoon to tell me the news that he thought we should consider following the advice, and I said, "Great, honey. Is that a part-time job?" I was thinking he meant state representative.

At the time, I was not very politically savvy at all. I hadn't been raised politically; I rarely read a newspaper, and I was very content just teaching and not being involved. But things were about to change.

CHAPTER THREE

Running for Congress
and Learning from Our Mistakes

*When picking a new colony location, female "scout bees" fly
out to search for potential sites, and report back to the colony,
with the famous waggle dance. As soon as enough worker bees
agree and imitate the waggle dance, a new nest area is decided.*

We felt called to join this race. Mike and I had met with several
close friends to talk through what running for office would mean,
what sacrifices we would need to make. We prayed about it and
felt we were supposed to run. At the time, I don't think we really
had any idea what running for Congress would entail. Campaigns
require a lot of time and a tremendous amount of money. We were
constantly traveling the eleven-county district attending as many
events as we could.

To run for Congress, Mike had to quit practicing law after he won the primary. He had been working at a downtown law firm where they didn't want him to be a candidate while he was working at the firm. The firm let him take a sabbatical and kept him on the payroll and I kept teaching second grade. We were very blessed to have the income to make this first run for Congress.

Our new home we had recently bought was outside of the district that included Mike's hometown of Columbus. So for him to run, we wanted to physically move into the district. We decided to keep our home outside of the district and let our campaign manager live there and rented a condo in the congressional district near the school where I was teaching. That was a tough move for me since we would be moving out of our first home that we owned and loved.

This would be our third home we would be moving to, the third of eighteen moves over the course of our political career. We adopted a scripture verse for that first campaign that we've needed to return to time and again over the years:

THOSE WHO CLING TO WORTHLESS IDOLS FORFEIT
THE GRACE THAT COULD BE THEIRS.

(Jonah 2:8)

I didn't want that house to become an idol for me, to hold us back from whatever God had in store for us. A few months before we had decided to run for Congress, we had put new flooring in the kitchen, and I was impatient with the drying time for the glue for the linoleum. I asked Mike to move the refrigerator back into place. He gently reminded me we were supposed to wait twelve hours. I really wanted to see the whole effect of the new floor with the fridge back against the wall. I urged him to go ahead and move it, and sure enough . . . the linoleum tore. I remember melting to the floor like the Wicked Witch of the West in *The Wizard of Oz*. I was so disappointed, but it was my own fault. The good thing that came from that was that I had a moment right then where I realized I was really making this home kind of an idol. The kitchen floor had become so important to me, I couldn't even wait twelve hours for the adhesive to dry.

But I have to be honest, moving out of the first home we owned was going to be a tough move. This required some soul-searching trust. This was going to require me to let go of this house. That little house had a great front porch where we hung a porch swing. We would sit out there in the evenings with our dog, Buddy, lying at our feet and reconnect at the end of the day. We loved our neighbors, and we were within walking distance of my family.

In the end, off we went. We found a place to rent in the district that was close to where I was teaching, and we let our campaign manager stay in that little home. We started campaigning and loving it. Mike ran on the theme "Get Congress Working Again." I didn't know a lot of details about politics, which was a concern of mine at first, but one of the things I learned right away was that I didn't need to know everything about every issue. I just needed to listen to people and take their concerns back to Mike. What I loved about meeting supporters, both financial donors and volunteers, was seeing their enthusiasm and concern for their community, state, and nation. This was a new world to me. And it was humbling to see so many people jump on board our team. Our campaign didn't have a lot of money, so we decided to bike the entire eleven-county district to get some earned media. This was during a drought in Indiana that summer, so we logged a lot of miles in the scorching heat. But it did earn us some news coverage.

Tragedy struck during that first campaign and it impacted us more than losing any election. Mike's dad passed away suddenly in April, right before the primary. It was a total blow that devastated the whole family. Ed had only been fifty-seven years old. He had been a key player in that first campaign, getting his friends on board. He told Mike that if he raised $30,000 all on his own, then Ed would enlist his friends to support Mike. He was a huge part of our lives and losing him was devastating.

I remember Mike going out in the field next to our condo for a long time one evening. When he came back in, he shared with me that he had needed to get mad at God for taking his dad. That was shocking to me. I questioned him about how he could think that he could get mad at God. But he explained that his relationship with the Lord is very honest, and he couldn't just pretend it was okay for God to let his dad die so suddenly. He had to get his feelings out. It was the first time I had ever heard anything like that. It really helped me to understand that my relationship with Christ is just that . . . a relationship. And like any relationship, it was important not to hold my feelings in, but to express them, even to God.

I was grateful that Mike and his dad had had some special moments going to meet with some of Ed's friends as we started our first campaign. But we missed him then and still do today. Every election, we think of him and how proud he would be of where his son is now—not just what he accomplished, but how he did it. And that first election is when we learned some key lessons on how *not* to do it.

We lost our first election, but the county official had been right . . . running is the best way to learn about running. My understanding of politics shifted, too. I now realized that a lot is at stake in every election. Issues matter, and it is important to be involved. This was a mantle I was comfortable wearing. Standing for our beliefs in limited government, faith, family, and freedom was worth it.

We knew we would run again, and we started right away. The second campaign was more difficult. We sold our first home that I had loved so much and bought a home in the congressional district. Campaign finance rules at the time specified the candidate is really the only person who doesn't get paid by the campaign. That can make it tough to support your family when you quit your job to devote your efforts full-time to campaigning. We had had the benefit of Mike's sabbatical salary during the first election season, but the law firm did not want Mike to run again while working at the firm. We weren't sure how we were going to make our finances work this time. We had just purchased a new home. Running for the House of Representatives requires many hours of fundraising because each individual could only give $2,500 per election cycle: $2,500 for the primary and $2,500 for the general. But advertising and running a campaign is very expensive. When Mike quit his job, we researched the campaign finance rules at the time and were informed that we could legally have the campaign pay for a few of our bills and report it on our campaign finance disclosure. We decided to do that to make up for part of Mike's salary as a lawyer that we would have to forfeit during the campaign. We sent out a press release to inform all of the newspapers in the district. No one wrote anything until the week before the election, and the headline read, "Mike Pence Diverts Campaign Funds for Personal Use."

The attack was hurtful, both to us personally, since we weren't trying to hide anything, and to the campaign. We knew it was legal and allowed, but it stung to have our name slandered like that. And happening the week before the election gave us no time to explain and defend ourselves. I wondered how regular everyday Americans could ever be able to run for office if they would have to quit their jobs to run? It was stunning to me to see how some of our supporters and volunteers immediately believed whatever they read in the paper about us, even though they had been campaigning with us for years.

This is one of the most difficult aspects of politics. The press can say whatever they want, and because it is in print or on TV, many people believe it is true. But for me personally, it was a good lesson to learn, and I was careful from then on to keep a distance between my personal life and the political world. I had read about how Nancy Reagan kept a wall of protection around her marriage to Ronald Reagan, not letting staff past the first room in their home at the ranch. I was starting to understand. It was a great lesson, really, because it helped me keep the political world at bay later when we had a family.

About the same time, we decided to run some very negative ads about our opponent that depicted a green cow belonging to our opponent, representing the fact that our opponent had sold his family farm for a nuclear waste dump. Another ad showed a sheikh saying how much he liked our opponent voting to get oil from Arab countries. Those ads also earned us some pretty bad press.

We lost that election, too, but we learned a lot in the process. I think at first we felt disappointed because we had sacrificed so much. But as Mike reflected more on the entire campaign, he was more disappointed that we hadn't used our opportunity to talk about the positive aspects of the conservative cause . . . we had only tried to tear down the opposition. We had squandered this moment and hurt our own reputation in the process.

Mike wrote an essay titled "Confessions of a Negative Campaigner," which was published in our local paper. It detailed how we realized that by negatively campaigning we had lost an opportunity to further conservative values. He framed it, and it hung in his congressional office years later to remind us of what was really important. We were humbled. We had been very arrogant and pretty full of ourselves. And what we've learned over the years is that God can't really use us if we are trying to make things happen on our own, for our own gain, and do things our way. We had wanted to help change Congress, to make it work more for the American people. Deep down we had good intentions, but we didn't really understand the workings of politics, the fact that there are a lot of really good people in Washington. We had been very judgmental. I remember years later hearing an acquaintance describe the members all walking down the steps of the Capitol after a vote as "suits." And it bothered me. They aren't just suits. These are husbands, wives, fathers, and mothers. They are people who are sacrificing a lot to serve. His comments reminded me of my own ignorance back in 1990 when we had assumed we would be the only positive thing in Washington if we won. We had a lot to learn. We had to learn the hard way that Mike and Karen Pence weren't going to be God's gift to Washington, D.C.

So we dusted off our bruised egos and left politics. Mike stayed involved with policy work running a statewide think tank, practiced law for a while, and later started a talk radio show.

CHAPTER FOUR

Our Dream Home

*Honeybees are not born with the knowledge about how to
make honey. Instead, older bees in the hive teach them.*

While we had been running for Congress, we had also been trying
to start our family. As anyone who has struggled with infertility
can relate, it can be a very emotional time. Lots of ups and downs.
Lots of infertility treatments and procedures. Lots of money. Lots
of heartbreak. It didn't matter that the doctor was telling me he
didn't know why I wasn't getting pregnant. The only thing he
could point to was sometimes my progesterone was on the low
side. But I still didn't have a baby, and I was in my early thirties, so
it was very discouraging. All I really ever wanted was to be a mom.
And it seemed like every time we found out we weren't pregnant,
some friend or family member was. I remember one family brunch
where my little niece looked up at me and said, "Auntie Karen,

why don't you have any babies?" I told her God hadn't given me a baby yet.

I had undergone several GIFT (gamete intrafallopian transfer) procedures. These are performed laparoscopically. Not a super difficult procedure, but definitely not comfortable. To prepare, the doctor gave me shots to take at home daily to make the ovaries produce extra eggs. This had the effect of making me look about four months pregnant for several weeks. We hadn't shared with anyone that we were doing all of this, so I was concerned my colleagues must suspect I was pregnant. I certainly looked it. None of my clothes fit, either. Then, after each procedure, we went through the heartache of knowing it was unsuccessful. Mike's dad reached out to him, thinking we were waiting to have kids. He said, "Michael, there's no easy time to have kids. Just remember they don't come out as teenagers." So we decided to let our parents know we were doing everything we could to start our family. In retrospect, I'm glad we shared that with Ed because he was gone before we had any children, so it is a comfort to know he was aware that we were trying.

After six years of infertility, which had seemed like forever (I was thirty-four now), I was home waiting for the latest lab result from my doctor to see if I was pregnant. Mike was on the road in northern Indiana and called to see if I had heard anything yet. I answered by saying, "Happy Father's Day!" He let out a "whooooo" on the other end. I was finally able to say those words to him. I remember laughing out loud at his reaction.

Mike will frequently tell people even now that he had given up on us having kids. I think it was just too painful to keep hoping. But he always gives me credit for never giving up. So it was a great moment! And I was finally going to be a mom. I could hardly believe it! Those years of trying to start our family had been difficult. Sometimes I wondered why God had put such a strong desire in my heart to have children if He wasn't going to bring me any. But then I would take solace in that same fact, that since the desire was so strong, I had to cling to the hope that He would fulfill that desire somehow, someway, someday. And if I truly believed that His ways are best and that He desires only the best for me, I could rest there. Later, reflecting on *when* He brought our family, I could then see His wisdom. The fact that our kids were so young when Mike finally did get elected made it much easier for them to move to Washington. If they had been teenagers when he got elected, it would have made for a much more difficult transition.

Over the years, I've come to realize that if I truly trust God, then I have to trust Him with everything, and putting that principle into daily practice has helped me stay calm through the storms. I'm not saying it is easy, and I'm certainly not saying I am good at trusting Him during difficult moments, but I am saying that when I finally let go and give Him the reins, He brings me a calm, "a peace that surpasses understanding" (Philippians 4:6).

Meanwhile, we also were on an adoption list, content to start our family however God wanted to bless us. While I was pregnant with Michael, we got a call that a young girl and her boyfriend were considering us to adopt their baby. But we also knew that there were four other couples they were considering who were hoping for that baby. Mike and I took a walk one night and both agreed that since I was pregnant, we should trust that God would bring this baby I was carrying to a healthy birth, and we took our name off of the list to allow one of the other couples to adopt this baby. We knew that the baby was a boy. I have shared this story with our own kids, and Michael never forgave me for not giving him a brother. We went on to have three kids in three years, with

Charlotte and Audrey following right behind Michael. Our family life was finally beginning.

Having finally realized our dream of having a family, I jumped into the role of being a mom with full force. I loved it, but it was exhausting! As anyone who has kids can relate to, it seems like you will never get another uninterrupted night's sleep, but the babies turn into toddlers, the toddlers turn into school-aged kids, and eventually you are sending your kids out the door to college or a career. I love *The Push* by David McNally, where he describes how the mama eagle needs to push her offspring out of the nest. He says, "Until her children discovered their wings, there was no purpose for their lives. Until they learned how to soar, they would fail to understand the privilege it was to have been born an eagle."

That "push" comes before you know it. I tell people the struggle with infertility made me a better mom. It didn't make me a better mom than other moms are, but I think it made me a better mom than I would have been if it hadn't been so difficult to have children. On days where my kids would drive me crazy—and believe me, there were plenty of those—I would remind myself that I almost didn't have this. And I would take a breath and thank God for this privilege. Because parenting is hard, but this was a role that He had brought to me, and He would help me through those tough days.

I decided to be a stay-at-home mom and not go back to teaching yet. I joined a little gym class with Michael when he was almost a year old. A few of the moms got together after class and decided to start a playgroup. Four of us, myself along with Kirstin Phillips, Jane Wainwright, and Jamie Broyles, stuck with it for many years, and I still get together with these moms three or four times a year. Over the next several years, the four of us had seventeen kids between us. It was quite a little group. We would meet once a week at a different person's home and just let the kids play. We divvied up the food each week and each brought something to help feed this brood. We had four categories. Meat and cheese, bread and chips and pretzels, fruit and dessert, and the hostess would provide plates and drinks. I still am drawn back to those days every time I have a turkey sandwich with real mayonnaise on white bread with pretzels. We went to the Children's Museum, the Indianapolis Zoo, Indianapolis Indians baseball games, parks, out to lunch to teach the kids how to behave at a restaurant, and on and on.

This group really became an outlet for me and my kids. Those years of life are so intense that it's important to share them with people going through the same struggles. My kids learned how to share and how to behave during outings. I remember once arriving at the zoo telling the other moms that if my kids didn't behave, we were heading home. Michael, Charlotte, and Audrey had been warned. I apologized to my friends, but explained I needed my kids to see me follow through if they misbehaved. And the threat had been issued before we left home. "If you can't behave, we will leave the zoo and come home."

As any mom knows, if you threaten, you had better follow through with it or you will never be taken seriously again. The morning had been rough just getting to the zoo, and I was pretty sure things were going to escalate. We got the stroller out, water bottles, snacks . . . we trudged through the parking lot to the entrance, got through the gate, and that's as far as we got. I can't remember exactly what happened, but sure enough . . . we headed home shortly after arriving.

As a new mom, I also started attending Mothers of Preschoolers, or MOPS, as it is typically called. I was so surprised when I joined and was informed that the moms of preschoolers bring all of the snacks, and everything starts at 9 a.m. I had no idea how I was going to get Michael, me, and now baby Charlotte anywhere by 9 a.m., especially with a snack in tow. But I learned that I could do it. The great thing about this group was that we all were in the same stage of life, so we understood if we showed up with Cheerios in our hair or two mismatched shoes. It was very comforting! We had a more experienced older mom share a Bible lesson, parenting tips, and a craft. It was so helpful to feel supported by other moms while the kids had a lesson as well. As my kids grew, we graduated from MOPS and started going to Bible Study Fellowship. Audrey, now five at this point, and I became MOPS helpers at our new church.

At one of the early MOPS meetings, a woman shared how she kept a prayer journal for her kids throughout their lives. I loved this idea. Over the next twenty-five years, I kept a prayer journal for each of my kids. Honestly, some years I was so busy, I only wrote an entry on their birthday. But I tried to take time to include highlights from their lives, moments even where I had prayed for their character or for God to show them His presence, or to highlight their gifts and achievements. They all knew I was writing in it, but they didn't get to read them until the night before they went to college, when I gave them a copy to take with them. It was always an emotional evening reading through it before they headed off. It was a great way to recap their lives up until that moment and to see God's faithfulness through the years.

It also gave them confidence as they saw confirmation of their gifts and strengths that had grown over their childhood. I kept writing in it until their weddings. They each now have the originals, and I have the copies to look back and remember. And of course, now I am keeping one for my granddaughters, Avery, Etta, and Elena! The prayers are simple. They read like a letter. "Dear Michael, Today you started first grade. Dad gave you some advice on his radio show. Keep the Lord in your heart, a good head on your shoulders, and mind your manners. You're going to do great. Tonight you could hardly sleep. Love, Mom."

I also chose a life verse for each of our kids when they were babies. Michael's is Psalm 40:1, "I waited patiently for the Lord, and He inclined to me and heard my cry." It used to be so difficult when I was a brand-new mom to hear Michael cry. So I researched verses about how God hears our cry. Charlotte's is Colossians 3:12, "Therefore, as God's chosen people, holy and dearly loved, clothe yourselves with compassion, kindness, humility, gentleness, and patience." I can still hear her little three-year-old voice reciting her verse before bed. Audrey's is Philippians 4:8, "Finally, Brothers, whatever is true, whatever is noble, whatever is right, whatever is pure, whatever is lovely, whatever is admirable—if anything is excellent or praiseworthy, think about such things." I painted a watercolor illustrating their verse and hung it in their rooms to remind them of God's promises. I had the sweetest gift from Michael and Sarah when they chose a verse for our first grandchild, Avery, and asked me to illustrate it to hang over her crib. When I visit them and get Avery up in the morning, she and I pause for a moment, and she wraps her little arm around my neck, and we start the day looking at her watercolor from her Kiki and saying her verse. Now with two more grandchildren recently born, I have had two more requests. It is the most tender thing to know my grandkids will have their own Kiki watercolor painted just for them with a verse their parents chose specifically for them to guide them through their lives.

When our kids were one, two, and three, we decided to build our dream home. It was quite a project, choosing everything for that home and making so many decisions during the process. (Yes, we had made another move in the meantime!) We built it not far from where we lived then. The day the driveway was poured, the kids each placed their hands in the wet concrete at the top of the drive to commemorate the occasion. (Those handprints are still there, and the current owners were kind enough to let us do a re-take photo with the kids putting their grown hands in the smaller concrete prints when they were in their late teens.) We created many memories in that home.

Mike had his radio show then from nine to twelve each morn-ing, syndicated all over Indiana. Because he worked from home in the afternoon, we designed the house to have a separate staircase from the garage to his office over the garage. We soundproofed that room so he could come home in the afternoons to work with-out the kids knowing he was there, and he wouldn't wake them up from their naps as he made his calls. I started my watercolor business, painting custom watercolors of my clients' homes in the afternoons during nap time.

This was a rich time in our lives. This was a mantle I loved wearing. Being a mom is my favorite role. I am grateful to be a mom. And I really immersed myself in being my kids' mom. I re-member Michael coming home from kindergarten the first week of school. He sat up on a stool at the island in the kitchen, I fixed him a toasted bagel, and I said, "Let me help you with your home-work." I was so excited to share in this. He looked at me seriously and said, "Mom . . . it's my responsibility." Lesson learned! Part of being a good mom is learning to let go and let them do things for themselves.

We thought this house would be our forever home. I had started teaching art a few hours each week at the kids' elementary school. I had started my custom home watercolor business and enjoyed showing my artwork at local art fairs. Mike's radio show was going great. He had even started a TV show and a TV special. Life was looking good. Our plan was going great . . . kids in school, we both had careers we loved, we had our new home, the American dream! But it's been my experience, and probably yours, too, that when your life seems to be going smoothly, that's usually when God puts it into a blender. And He had such different plans for us, plans way beyond what we ever could have imagined or planned for. Amazing plans, not easy . . . but amazing.

CHAPTER FIVE

Deciding to Run Again

If a queen honeybee is taken out of the hive,
within fifteen minutes, the rest of the colony knows it!

Several years went by and we were content. We had three small kids, Mike had a fulfilling job, and we were in a good place as a family. But then the congressional seat Mike had run for twice before and lost—became open.

Mike's name recognition was sky-high due to the radio show, and his listeners knew exactly where he stood on the issues. He also had great relationships with the donors who had supported us so many years before. Many people had been approaching him to see if he would be interested in running again for the congressional seat.

So we felt we needed to at least consider running again as a possibility.

This is not what we had anticipated. Life was comfortable. We had let that dream go. Perhaps this was why God brought it back into our lives again. Because now, it wasn't our idea, our ambition leading us. It was more a sense of service and calling. But in reality, this would mean tremendous sacrifices for our family. This would entail Mike stopping his radio show since that would be free advertising if he became a candidate, which isn't allowed. This would also mean moving from our dream home that we had only lived in for three years, because the congressional district lines had now been redrawn to exclude our home, even though this neighborhood had been in the district when Mike ran previously. Another move! In the back of my mind, that old verse from the very first campaign kept reminding me, "Those who cling to worthless idols forfeit the grace that could be theirs." Was I making this new home an idol? Mike was turning forty that summer, too. It was a lot to think about. Could God really be calling us to do this all again? Was He asking me to be a political wife with three small children?

I consider myself a risk taker by nature. I used to have a motorcycle before I met Mike, and I got my pilot's license in my early twenties, and I've gone skydiving. I like to rise to the challenge, whatever might come up. But I initially had some real concerns when faced with this big change in our family's life. This time it was different than when we had run for Congress before. We had children . . . *What would it be like to raise them in Washington? What would this decision mean to them, to their lives?* I ultimately came to the conclusion that if we ran and won, this challenge of living in Washington would be part of their life tapestry, that I didn't need to shelter them from life's adventures. And we would be going together. This could be a real opportunity to show them an example of their parents answering a call from God and following our dreams. If we didn't win, it would still be a lesson for them in how to go in the direction God is calling you. It's hard to do, and it's hard to know what that is sometimes, but I believe God will show us His plan for our lives if we listen to and pursue Him. But we still both didn't feel clarity yet. This was a lot to consider.

For Mike's fortieth birthday, I surprised him with an outdoor party complete with a tent, dance floor, and a DJ. I had saved all of my watercolor painting income to give him a gift of a family trip to a dude ranch in Colorado because he loves to ride horses. One afternoon near the end of our stay at the ranch, Mike and I took a ride by ourselves up to the top of a bluff in Roosevelt National Forest. The whole week, we both had been struggling with the decision of whether or not to run for Congress again. We had been thinking, praying, talking through what it would mean. We got off our horses and sat on a ledge on the side of the bluff. Mike said, "We've got to make a decision. Time is running out."

We had been to this rodeo before, pun intended. We understood the demands of campaigning and the additional demands of raising the funds necessary, the time commitment, the financial commitment. We had weighed the pros and cons, discussed it at length, and prayed extensively. But he was right. It was time.

Mike is a romantic at heart. As we were sitting on that ledge we looked out and saw two red-tailed hawks. They were rising on the wind, letting the wind's current lift them higher and higher.

"See those two hawks? Those are like us," Mike said.

"Well, if those two hawks are like us, then I think we should run. But this time we should run like the hawks," I replied. "We should step off this cliff and make ourselves available to God. And this time instead of ambition driving us, we should allow God to lift us up to wherever He wants to use us with No Flapping." And right then and there, in Roosevelt National Forest, we made the decision—and "No Flapping" has been our mantra ever since.

Every new staff member at some time hears this story. They understand this is our approach to decision making. We want to be open to God's calling and His leading in our lives. We don't want to be forcing our own wills and desires into the equation when making major life decisions. And somehow when we have had to make these monumental decisions in our lives, it's His peace that seems to always confirm our choices. While trying to discern His will, there is always a lot of uncertainty, bordering on unease or anxiety. But once we have weighed all of the options, the pros and cons, counseled with other advisors, prayed and asked others to pray, there comes the moment a decision needs to be made. And once that decision is made, His peace settles in and we move forward. Red-tailed hawks have become kind of symbolic to us. Years later, a reporter at the White House captured a male and female red-tailed hawk sitting on a ledge at the Eisenhower Executive Office Building, part of the White House complex. Mike showed me the photo, and I had it printed and framed for him as a Christmas present. It still sits in his home office.

So we were running. . . . again. I realized my job was to be willing to go wherever God was asking me to go. I had to trust Him. I needed to be willing to serve. We had no idea if we would win, but we saw this as an opportunity to redeem our reputation and run an entirely positive campaign solely focused on the issues. We felt God was giving us a second chance to prove we really had learned our lesson.

We won the primary. This meant we put our dream home that we had built on the market and rented a home in the district. We didn't buy yet because we wanted to buy once the new district lines were set. This was now our first campaign with kids in tow.

Fortunately, the kids loved campaigning. We went to fairs, fund-raisers, and speeches with them and made it fun and a family affair. We would take their jammies with us, and I taped an old TV/VCR player to the armrests in the front seat of our minivan with duct tape. I purchased an outlet adapter that we could plug the TV into, that plugged into our cigarette lighter. (This was before TVs were standard drop-down accessories in minivans.) We would pick out one of our videos before leaving for the campaign event and put it in the car. Sometimes we would stop for an ice cream cone on the way home. Many of our supporters would make sure they had an area in their home where the kids could go and play or have a hot dog while we mingled at a reception. As the kids grew older, we made a point to let them know they never were required to campaign with us, but they were always welcome.

Election night 2000 included lots of friends, supporters, and family. Everyone gathered at a big theater in Anderson, Indiana. Amid loud applause, as music played, Mike and I and the kids walked down a long aisle with supporters on each side and took the stage. God had allowed us to win. We were pretty pumped!

One of the themes of this third campaign had been family values, so we had made it public we intended to keep our family together. After trying for so long to have a family, we wanted to be together. Whether we succeeded or failed, this was a journey we were going to take as a family. We knew being a congressman is a two-year job so we might just be in Washington for two years, and we wanted to make the most of it. We wanted our kids to experience it all. We might be packing up and heading back to Indiana after any election cycle. It was important to us that we teach them how to take risks and follow their dreams, how to trust God.

While Mike was in Congress, I was asked several times to speak at Tables of Christmas events at local churches in Indiana. These are wonderful affairs where table hosts decorate their tables with a different Christmas theme and invite their friends to the event. One year my topic was, "Teach us to number our days, that we may gain a heart of wisdom" (Psalm 90:12). Life is short, and we aren't promised tomorrow. I wanted my kids to learn that every day is precious. They in return taught us a lot about resiliency. They just went with the flow. But now I needed to find a home and a school for us in D.C. And I adopted a new verse for moving that has comforted me many times. In Deuteronomy 1:30–33, God is reprimanding the Israelites for not trusting him, even though He has been there for them.

THE LORD YOUR GOD, WHO IS GOING BEFORE YOU, WILL FIGHT FOR YOU, AS HE DID FOR YOU IN EGYPT, BEFORE YOUR VERY EYES, AND IN THE WILDERNESS. THERE YOU SAW HOW THE LORD YOUR GOD CARRIED YOU, AS A FATHER CARRIES HIS SON, ALL THE WAY YOU WENT UNTIL YOU REACHED THIS PLACE. IN SPITE OF THIS, YOU DID NOT TRUST IN THE LORD YOUR GOD, WHO WENT AHEAD OF YOU ON YOUR JOURNEY, IN FIRE BY NIGHT AND IN A CLOUD BY DAY, TO SEARCH OUT PLACES FOR YOU TO CAMP AND TO SHOW YOU THE WAY YOU SHOULD GO.

I love the image of God carrying us, as a father carries his son. But my favorite part is the fact that God went ahead to search out places for them to camp. Many more moves would come in the future, although I was unaware of it at the time. During this big move to D.C., I started claiming that verse, that God would go ahead and find us a place to camp! And I would trust Him.

CHAPTER SIX

Raising a Family in D.C.

*Honeybees typically journey around three miles away
from the hive looking for nectar and pollen.*

What I realized fairly soon after our arrival was that moving our family to Washington was not the norm. There really wasn't much of a support system established. Many spouses come to Washington for special events, but most decide to stay in their home state, and those who move their whole family are few and far between. There are several reasons for this, of course. Lots of them have their own careers back in their own districts or perhaps they are caring for elderly parents or maybe it's not a good time to move their kids. Every congressional family has to make the decision that is right for their family. Not very many choose to come to Washington.

It was difficult to leave our family, friends, and life behind in Indiana, but I knew that God was calling us to keep our family close through what would be several years of Him stretching us, and stretching me in particular—placing me in a new role.

It isn't easy to take up the mantle and answer God's call on our lives, but I have found that when we do so, He will honor it.

We never forgot our roots, but we didn't want our kids to think they were celebrities in Indiana with their dad being a congressman. At their school in Northern Virginia, there were other congressional kids, kids whose parents worked at the White House, the Pentagon, cabinet undersecretaries, etc. Their experiences really weren't much different than their friends.

Parenting is hard enough, and I couldn't imagine trying to parent with Mike in another city all week. For us, being together every night was important. But being together and living in Washington meant our kids were exposed to some very difficult situations on the one hand, and some amazing once-in-a-lifetime experiences on the other.

During orientation week shortly after the election, I went house-hunting with a former congressional spouse who was a Realtor. I told her we wanted to rent the first term and then buy if Mike got reelected. Since we would be moving again if we got reelected, we decided to try to find a private Christian school so that the kids wouldn't have to move schools again if we won the second term. I wanted this transition to be as smooth as I could make it for our kids.

The market then was very tight, but we found a home in South Arlington to rent. My mother and I flew out in December to meet the moving truck and get the house all set up for the kids. We also were planning to have Mike's "Thank You Reception" for friends and supporters at our home the day he would be sworn in, so I needed to get everything set up. I was getting pretty good at this moving thing!

This same spouse took me to a school that another former congressional spouse's children had attended. I went inside and said I was looking to enroll my children in January in kindergarten and first and third grades. The office manager explained to me that the school was full, but I could go on a wait list. I agreed to do that, and mentioned that I would just homeschool to finish the remainder of this school year, explaining that I was a teacher, and was the part-time art teacher at my kids' school in Indiana. After nine years of being home full-time, I had been helping out as the art teacher at the kids' Indiana school that year. It had been a good transition back into teaching and helped me be involved in the kids' school as well.

She looked at me and said, "You are a licensed elementary art teacher? We need an art teacher. If we hire you, your kids would be admitted in each grade."

Immediately, this felt like a total "God thing." I felt God was orchestrating this. Not only would I have my own career and identity in Washington, but I would be doing what I loved, would know my kids' friends and teachers, and would quickly have a community. Plus the job was part-time. I taught at Immanuel Christian School for the full twelve years while Mike was in Congress and then again for three years as second lady. I was ready to go back to teaching again. I looked forward to getting to know all of these new students, teaching them art. God was giving me a place where I could just be "me," not "Karen Pence, Mike Pence's wife." This was something that God gave me again and again throughout our political life. There were opportunities—either through my initiatives or with my own job and career—where I was able to be myself and glorify God in the gifts He had given me. When Mike was vice president, I returned to this same school to teach art again a few days a week. It gave me the opportunity to really do something I loved and have my own career.

One of the benefits of our kids living in Washington was their exposure to our country's history. They had such a better understanding of our government than I did at their age. As children of a member of Congress, they were allowed to go on the floor of the House Chamber with their dad. They were allowed to be with him as he voted. Spouses are not allowed, but a member's children are. It was quite a privilege for them. They all also served as Senate pages during the summer after their junior year in high school. Living in Washington was a fantastic experience for our kids as they grew into the people that they are today.

As I said before, our kids were very involved in the campaign. Our son, Michael, seemed to be especially invested, not that the girls weren't, but I knew he would be very disappointed if we lost, and being older, it might be more difficult for him to leave his friends in Indiana. Due to the timing of our elections, we were moving in the middle of a school year. So, I told him that win or lose, right after the election, he could have a bearded dragon lizard. And I was determined to keep my promise. We drove the minivan out to D.C. right after Christmas. I still remember rounding a turn and the kids seeing the view of our nation's capitol from the George Washington Parkway for the first time. It was an exciting moment. We pulled up to the house, and they got to explore their new rooms and get adjusted. Meanwhile, I got in the car and headed all over Northern Virginia to several pet stores in search of a bearded dragon on Day 1 as I had promised. After a long search, I headed home with "Gollum" (as Michael named him . . . "Bob" for short). We had Bob for about ten years until he passed away from old age. I think I was the one who was most emotional at his little backyard burial.

We also had Buddy, a Cocker/Lab mix that I had given Mike as a Christmas present our first year of marriage and Madeline, Audrey's cat. That first term, Charlotte adopted an orange-and-white cat named Pickle. Pickle was scared of everything and would hide in the rental house basement rafters for hours. But Charlotte was so patient with her and loved her and loved her and loved her until she became one of the friendliest cats we ever had.

We were quickly faced with some challenging trials when we got to D.C., but we knew that God had called us here and He would be with us. In March of that same year, I was shocked when two people suddenly unlocked our front door and walked right into our rental home while I was preparing dinner. They didn't even knock. Mike wasn't home at the time, and I was scared and confused. I came to realize after a few minutes that this was a Realtor with the new owner of our rental. The Realtor explained that the previous owner had let the mortgage lapse, and it had gone into foreclosure without us even knowing. The new owner told me right then that the rent was going up a thousand dollars a month, and I needed to get rid of my dog that week. When Mike called this man, the conversation became quite heated, and we realized we needed to get out of that house.

So once again, I knew I needed to trust that God would go before us and search out a place for us to camp. We could not afford a thousand dollars more a month, and we were definitely not getting rid of Buddy, who had been part of our family since our first year of marriage. I must admit this was a little daunting. The market then in the Washington/Northern Virginia area was very tight, especially for a rental home. But trusting God, later that same week,

Audrey and I were driving around to try to find another rental. We saw a home up on a hill with a "For Rent" sign out in the front yard. We pulled up the hill and got out and saw the owner in the yard. I explained our predicament. We signed a lease that next day, and some amazing volunteers and friends helped us move to the new home that very weekend, wooden swing set, backyard play fort, and all. The timing of the whole move within one week was truly a miracle! It was in moments like these where I could see God's hand of protection on us. I was learning that if I just trusted Him, He truly would take care of us.

I experienced this again and again. One afternoon at that house, while Mike was campaigning in Indiana, I went upstairs and happened to look out the window and saw two people loading our dog, Buddy, into their car. It was a miracle that I happened to look out the window just at that moment. I ran downstairs and started shouting at them. They explained that they had found her lying on the ground at the foot of our hill without her collar. Somehow, while hooked up to her outside chain, she had wiggled out of her collar and had a heart attack and fell down the hill. I grabbed her up into my arms, yelled at the kids to jump in the van, and raced her to the vet. Fortunately, we just barely caught Mike by phone visiting his mom in Columbus, Indiana, during the one hour when he was reachable. This was before cell phones. We called him from the vet's phone, and he stayed on the line as we all tearfully said our goodbyes to Bud. It was a heartbreaking moment, but I was so grateful I had looked out the window at exactly the right time to be able to run and get her and for all of us to be able to say goodbye instead of always wondering what had happened to her.

We wanted life to be as normal as possible while still treasuring some of the amazing opportunities afforded us due to Mike's position.

Mike's routine in Congress was to go home to Indiana every other weekend for meetings, town halls, fundraisers, and political dinners. Once the district lines had been set, we moved from the rental in Indiana to a little three-bedroom home we purchased on the outskirts of Columbus. It was near the Flatrock River, where the kids loved to swim. Mike liked to say he could see "six miles and count eighteen barns from the backyard." One of the first things we did to that house was to install a flagpole. Mike loves having a flagpole. We used that flagpole in a commercial one year, with Michael and Mike raising the flag with the sunrise behind them. It was really nice owning a home in Indiana again.

Frequently, Mike would take one of the kids home to Indiana with him for the weekend, and they would make an adventure of it, introducing their dad at speeches and greeting supporters. Now that the kids were getting older, though, we reinforced again that going forward they would never have to campaign or attend any political or official events unless they wanted to. For the most part, I think we were able to maintain that boundary. We believed in raising them to think for themselves, and that made for some pretty passionate discussions in the years ahead. Our kids have their own beliefs and opinions, and that's the way we wanted it. But they did enjoy filming the campaign commercials every two years.

At that time in Congress, there were annual bipartisan congressional family retreats. These were great opportunities for congressional families to make friends across the aisle. Our kids loved these retreats. Usually, a whole resort or hotel would be reserved, and there were Capitol Police throughout, so our kids were safe to explore their surroundings on their own. It gave them a lot of freedom. There were also family retreats for each political party. All of these retreats allowed our kids to be around other kids experiencing life as a child of a member of Congress. Spouses also had an opportunity to share their experiences with each other. The president would usually make an appearance and graciously allow each family to get photos. At one of the first retreats, Michael was waiting patiently with a three-by-five card to get George W. Bush's autograph. The girls didn't have one.

When President Bush came up, he said, "Are you gonna share that with your sisters? Here, I'll sign it three times and you can share it."

Then he looked at Mike and jokingly said, "Pence, I don't want to see that on eBay!"

We still have that card, with all three signatures . . . uncut!

Life settled into a fairly normal routine.

I purchased a little book that listed lots of great activities to do in D.C., and we tried to do as many as we could. We would walk around Hains Point and climb on *The Awakening* sculpture before it was moved to National Harbor, in Maryland. Created by J. Seward Johnson Jr., *The Awakening* is a giant bronze sculpture depicting a bearded man emerging from the sand. Just his chest and limbs are exposed. His torso remains still in the sand as he struggles to "awaken." We went to special places like Mount Vernon and learned about where our first president lived. We road-tripped to Monticello to learn about Jefferson. We went to a Nationals game and the Spy Museum and Ford's Theatre. We went to Baltimore, Annapolis, New York City, Philadelphia, skied in Pennsylvania, etc. We even Rollerbladed together along the National Mall in Washington, D.C., which proved to be much more difficult because the sidewalks are often composed of a pebble composite, but we made the most of it and had fun anyway. We tried to do everything available in Washington and close to Washington, knowing any election cycle we might be moving back to Indiana, and our time in D.C. could be over. When Ivanka Trump later asked me for tips on raising kids in Washington, D.C., I gave her my well-worn dog-eared book, encouraging her to use it as much as she could.

Many times, we would head downtown to the Capitol and bring Mike dinner and eat on the House steps or meet him across from the Capitol at Tortilla Coast, our favorite Mexican restaurant. Or he would head home for dinner or a soccer or lacrosse game and then head back to the Hill for votes. The first summer, we decided to have the kids and me go to Indiana for a long stretch to campaign while Mike stayed in D.C. for the appropriations votes. The debates on those votes always entailed long weeks and late nights. That summer was difficult for all of us; after that tough summer, we decided to stay with him in D.C. the next summer and wait to travel to Indiana during the August recess with him as a family. Many times, he would fly out first, and we would make the ten-hour drive with all of the pets and meet him at our home in Indiana. I love a road trip! I'd get up at four in the morning, load all the pets and kids into our van, and drive ten hours to meet Mike, who was already there. I'd put my headphones in and listen to a book on tape, and the kids would sleep. Usually they didn't wake up until around ten in the morning, and we'd stop at McDonald's. By then I only had about four hours left. I loved driving home. We'd always cheer and honk when we crossed over the Indiana line. Still do.

After Mike got reelected the first time, we realized that for financial reasons, we needed to purchase a home in Northern Virginia. I couldn't believe what houses cost in Virginia! The market was very tight, and most homes were selling right away above asking price. We had looked at many homes and were getting discouraged. The homes in our price range also seemed to need a lot of work. One night Mike was in Indiana, and I was in Virginia looking through the local Arlington neighborhood paper. I saw a home that looked like it was just barely in our price range, a three-bedroom, one-and-a-half-bathroom home with an unfinished basement. This home would mean all five of us would share a bathroom, and it didn't have a garage or even a dishwasher, but I decided to call the Realtor to inquire. The Realtor said a deal had just fallen through, and if I wanted to see the house the next morning and could offer full price, it could be ours. I called Mike in Indiana. He said to go for it. So I made an offer without him even seeing the house. But that house was meant to be ours. After so many moves, I continued to cling to the verse Deuteronomy 1:33, where Moses says the Lord went before the Israelites "to search out places for you to camp."

We moved in over the Christmas break, and I hung some drywall in the basement myself to try to improve it, and we took out some cabinets in the kitchen to add a dishwasher. That house was on a curved street, meaning it had very little traffic, and every single house on that street looked exactly the same. There were twenty-two kids on our street, and our basketball goal in front of our house was like a magnet. It was a special place for us to raise our kids—and we had great neighbors!

I remember when Hurricane Isabel hit Washington, D.C., in September 2003. Mike wasn't in D.C. at the time, and for safety, the kids and I slept in the basement. Unfortunately, a tree fell across our neighbor's car (no one was hurt) and blocked the street for several days. The street was without power, so we all brought out our grills and food that would otherwise spoil and had a big cookout block party.

It was at this house where we surprised Michael with our next dog, a two-year-old rescue beagle named Maverick. Maverick was very independent and had a mind of his own. But he was dearly loved by all of the neighborhood kids. About the same time, Madeline, Audrey's kitty, became very ill. We took her home to Indiana to our vet there, who told us she was suffering, and it was time.

Audrey wanted to bury Madeline at the Indiana house, so we had a little ceremony and placed her under the butterfly bush. Audrey's new kitty, Oreo, was actually there for the service. It was a sad moment, but the new kitten helped all of us feel better. Oreo made the long drive back to D.C. to her new home with us.

We tried to participate in whatever was going on at the Capitol that involved families. One week, we received an invitation to attend "Pet Night" on the Hill. Well, we thought, this is great! We are "pet people"! Of course we will attend Pet Night! So we loaded up our dog, Buddy, our cats, Pickle and Madeline, and of course, Bob, the bearded dragon. Up the steps we walked with three leashes and a shoe box. Boy, were we excited! But as you may have already guessed, Pet Night is not about bringing your pets to the Capitol. ("You're not in Kansas anymore, Dorothy!") Wow! Maybe we hadn't thought this through. Here we were in a reception with lobbyists from all of the major pet companies and I think it was the dog from *Men in Black*, posing for pictures on a large podium. We made the best of it, with one cat coughing up a hairball while the dog was pulling me toward the door. We still enjoyed ourselves, even though we felt like the Beverly Hillbillies. Mike had to head back for votes, and I remember the dog literally pulling me so hard, I fell facedown. But we made it home and decided we needed to read invitations a little more carefully going forward. It was a little humbling to show up as the only family with pets, but I knew this is where God wanted us to be, and He would guide us.

Obviously, living in the nation's capital wasn't without its challenges and we were met with many challenging situations early on. Mike likes to say that the safest place to be is in the center of

God's will. So we learned more and more to trust God in some of the dangerous situations in which we found ourselves. The first office Mike had was one of the offices attacked with anthrax, a powder that can kill on contact. As soon as we were made aware that our office was affected, our amazing staff carefully reconstructed the visitor log for the past week to alert all visitors to begin a regimen of Cipro, which is a strong antibiotic. Mike and I began taking it as well, and watched our kids closely for any signs that they needed to start medication. Thankfully, no one from our office was affected, but we grieved the loss of life that had occurred from this senseless attack.

This incident was a reminder of the risks involved in being a member of Congress and living in our nation's capital.

Teaching at my kids' school allowed me to be present for any emergency that might arise. Not only was I there for all of the kids' activities, but I also was at the school when Michael broke his collarbone in fourth grade, so I was able to rush him to the hospital. This was one of those times I was grateful we were near Mike, and he came right to the hospital from the Hill. I was also at school on the morning of September 11, 2001. One of Charlotte's gerbils had passed away that same week. And the teacher assistant in her classroom had told me the day before that Charlotte had been upset by it. The woman walked into my art room where I was prepping for the day and said, "Do you know what's happening?" I said, "Oh, is Charlotte still upset about Henry [her gerbil]?" It was then that I was informed about the planes that had flown into the twin towers of the World Trade Center in New York. I immediately went down to the teachers' lounge, where several of us started to pray. Shortly after, we heard that the Pentagon had also been hit. Many of the families at our school had parents who worked in D.C. at the White House, the Capitol, and the Pentagon. At that time, Mike had a BlackBerry, but I didn't. An announcement was made over the intercom, and not wanting our kids to get alarmed, I rushed to peek into all of my kids' classrooms to say, "Dad is okay." But in reality, I didn't know if he was.

As parents started arriving to get their children and take them home, one of the school secretaries and I made a plan that I would use the walkie-talkie out on the sidewalk to tell her what parents were pulling up, and she could call those kids from their classrooms so that we didn't have panic in the halls. At around 11 a.m., once the school had basically been emptied, I went to a phone and started trying to reach Mike. It took several attempts because all of the phone lines were jammed, but I finally reached him, and learned he was with leadership across the street from the Capitol. The kids and I headed home in a huge traffic jam and could see the smoke billowing in the distance from the Pentagon. Just hours before, we had driven right by it on our way to school. In the days that followed, we would drive by it again and again, with the black hole in the middle and the American flag draped beside it. We would witness each day how it was built again and put back together.

I also vividly remember the D.C. snipers. The snipers had randomly singled out and killed several people around the Washington, D.C., area. This was a time when people were afraid to be outside and exposed. Our son, Michael, had asked me if I was careful when I went into the grocery. He was worried about his mom. I assured him I was being very careful. One evening, Charlotte and I ran an errand to the local Home Depot. Little did we know the snipers were going to hit that parking lot the very next day. They may have even been scouting the area as we shopped. That really hit home the next day when we learned of the attack, especially since a woman from Columbus, Indiana, had been killed by the snipers in that parking lot. Such a senseless and tragic act.

These were scary times for everyone, and God was asking us to trust Him and His will every day, but in the midst of these challenges, we also had many amazing experiences living in Washington, D.C. It was always a privilege to go to the State of the Union, inaugurations, and to be able to take visiting constituents through the White House on any given day. I never lost my appreciation for where we were living and what a privilege it was. Every time I would drive into the Hill in the evening for an event or to pick up Mike, I marveled at the beauty of Washington with all of the monuments lit.

Living in D.C. was an amazing experience, but it was hard. I knew we weren't doing it alone, though. God was with us. He placed people in our path to support, encourage, and, most importantly, pray for us along the way. I attended the congressional spouse Bible study in the Capitol, and during Mike's years in Congress, friends and family asked me how they could pray for us, so I started a group email describing some prayer requests we had for us and members of Congress. Recipients told me they would forward the requests to their own prayer list, and the email ended up going to thousands of people. I sent it out about every week or two, and those prayers sustained us for sure! That email confirmed my conviction of the power of prayer.

Even though other congressional spouses became more involved in clubs and functions, I felt called to be where I was—a mom, a teacher, a carpooler, and a spectator at my kids' games, plays, and concerts. There were still plenty of official functions I attended, including the First Lady's Luncheon, which was hosted every year by the spousal Congressional Club, and of course, the

White House Congressional Christmas Ball and the White House Congressional Family Picnic. My girls were junior hostesses in the fashion show at the First Lady's Luncheon and later, at the urging of a friend, I would start my own Indiana First Lady's Luncheon as first lady of Indiana to raise money for charities all over my state. God was going before me and paving the way.

God also began showing me ways He wanted me to serve—not just while Mike was in Congress, but how I would end up serving in my roles in the future. A chance conversation would lead to an opportunity years later.

Around 2005, we had been invited to a behind-the-scenes tour of Disneyland in California by a lobbyist for Disney, Preston Padden. During the tour, he was introducing us to some of the animators. These amazingly talented artists were sharing lots of stories about some of the movies they were working on.

We were all fascinated, and I started a conversation with one such animator by saying, "I'm an elementary art teacher. Watching you at work, I'm wondering if I should focus on digital drawing with my students?" He assured me it was my job to still teach the fundamentals of drawing first.

Afterward, Preston said to me, "Karen, I didn't know you were an art teacher. I have a program back in D.C. that I think you would be very interested in."

Once we were back in D.C., he invited me to observe Tracy's Kids, an art therapy program for children with cancer. It was the first time I'd heard of art therapy, and I was enthralled. The lobby at Georgetown Lombardi Comprehensive Cancer Center displayed paint, clay, easels, and all types of art supplies. I observed young cancer patients focusing on their art projects and the creative process. They appeared to be oblivious to the tubes attached to them, and I later learned that many of these patients, once they return home, ask when they can come back to the hospital to do work with the art therapists. *Clearly*, I thought, *there is something to this.*

I was asked to join the Tracy's Kids congressional spouse steering committee and went around trying to tell anyone who would listen about this wonderful healing tool: art therapy. I would later go on to serve on their board. Over the years, as I have learned more and more about art therapy, I am amazed at how God created the brain and how these therapists use the knowledge that the brain is malleable to help their clients.

One example of this was the story of a young teen who was angry that he had cancer. He wanted nothing to do with the art therapy program at first. Tracy Councill, who heads up the Tracy's Kids program at Lombardi, shared with me that she patiently offered different art opportunities day after day. She waited for him to be ready. And one day, she showed him the potter's wheel. She demonstrated how to create a piece of pottery. He started creating that day. And as he added to his pieces of pottery over the course of his time there, the stack of completed pieces represented to him his healing journey in a tangible form.

Tracy's Kids became near and dear to my heart, and I became interested in researching whether Riley Hospital for Children in Indiana had an art therapy program. A friend, Bill Stephan, connected me to the then–chief executive officer of Riley, Dr. Ora Pescovitz, who explained that a group of women, many who were former art teachers, had just organized a group to raise money to hire an art therapist there. These were amazing women. Most art therapist positions need to be outside funded so they don't take away from hospital funds. I joined their cause and after about two and a half years, I was ecstatic once we had finally raised enough to cover the art therapist's salary and supplies.

During this time, God was also preparing our kids for what they would be called to do in the future. I can clearly see His hand at work in each of their lives.

One example of this, which our kids always enjoyed, was appearing in public service announcements. The National Association of Broadcasters would set up a studio and invite congressional families to record a PSA. The PSA was 90 percent completed, but each person reading for the PSA could read from the teleprompter to complete the final message of the ad. This way, the ads could be personalized to fit any congressional family participating. These would then air on TV and radio in the congressperson's home district. We thought it was a good way for our kids to do something that helped others, and it brought them into this political life in a fun way on their own terms. They never had to do the PSAs, but they wanted to, and it was fun to do them all together. And they all did great. Even today, we will use some of the catchphrases we memorized from those ads. Michael did one focused on physical fitness and we still tease him, saying, "Next time take the stairs . . . ," a phrase from the ad he recorded. At eight years of age, Audrey was especially adept at her recording. Some of the organizers saw her ad, and she was invited to present the award to the winner of the children's television programming at the National Broadcasters Association's annual dinner gala. The keynote speaker was Laura Bush, and the emcee was Bob Schieffer of CBS. I will never forget Audrey, an eight-year-old, dressed in her blue silk dress, standing on a wooden block so she could see over the podium and beginning, "Thank you, Mr. Schieffer, I'm delighted to be here . . ." And now, twenty years later, she is a poised young attorney.

In Washington, our kids attended the Christian elementary school where I taught through the eighth grade. They then transitioned to the public high school, where they had a typical high school career, with proms, sports, plays, etc. There was a great career center at that school where Michael was able to begin taking aviation classes in high school, and he discovered his love for flying. He majored in professional flight at Purdue, and is now an F-35 fighter pilot in the Marine Corps. Charlotte took film classes, loved them, and majored in digital cinema at DePaul University. Audrey was very involved in theater in high school, and went to Northeastern University in Boston for her undergraduate degree. During our kids' high school years, Mike led a Bible study for Michael and three of his friends at our house every Sunday night. The other moms would bring a meal for the guys; the boys would spend an hour or so skateboarding or playing basketball, have dinner in the basement (which by then we had finished and added another bedroom and full bath), and then do a Bible study with Mike.

Mike and I also made sure to prioritize our marriage and do fun things together. We have always loved walking together. It is a way for us to get away from our phones, kids, commitments, and focus on each other for twenty to thirty minutes each day. It is a way for us to reconnect. We're not runners, but we enjoy walking. Mike and I were invited to walk in a marathon by our sister-in-law, Denise Pence, who has done several marathons, and her husband, Gregory. They invited us to walk with them in the Marine Corps Marathon since Mike's brother is a Marine. We had done several of the Indianapolis 500 Mini-Marathons over the years, so we decided to go for it.

The Marine Corps Marathon is held in D.C. every fall. It's probably not the best marathon for rookies like us to do since roads in our nation's capital are closed during the marathon, meaning there are time restrictions. You need to "beat the bridge" over the Potomac by a certain time or you are put on a bus, and the marathon is over for you. For that reason, we trained pretty hard for this, not wanting to be put on a bus . . . and we made it! I think we were almost the last two people to finish, but it was a real sense of accomplishment. However, I do remember telling Denise we would never do that again . . . Years later, when Mike was vice president, our son, Michael, who is now a Marine himself, ran this same marathon. And we all came out to cheer him on!

We also wanted our kids to experience historical moments and take the time to appreciate the ways our country has grown. They joined us when Mike was invited by the late John Lewis to mark the forty-fifth anniversary of Bloody Sunday. Our family marched with him and several other members of Congress across the Edmund Pettus Bridge in Selma, Alabama. Our kids accompanied us as we stood along the street in Washington, paying tribute to Ronald Reagan as his caisson rolled past. We enjoyed July Fourth on the mall, attended the lighting of the congressional Christmas tree, and celebrated Audrey's eighth birthday party, climbing the 365 steps all the way up to the top of the dome of the Capitol Building. Our kids also participated in missions trips and volunteer opportunities; Michael went to Guatemala and the Dominican Republic while in college; Charlotte volunteered at a camp in Indiana after college; and Audrey ministered to the homeless right in Washington, D.C.

We were trying to do our best as parents while still serving our state in Congress. And God had richly blessed us. We had experienced that grace that the verse in Jonah had promised. "Those who cling to worthless idols forfeit the grace that could be theirs." As we neared the twelve-year mark in Congress, Mike was approached by some supporters to try a run for the presidency, yet other supporters thought he should run for the open governor's seat in Indiana. I remember one friend observing to us that it seemed that most of the support and enthusiasm was behind running for governor. She said that the runway lights were all lit for that path and not necessarily for the presidency.

Michael said to Mike, "Dad, I know you could run now and be a great president, but I don't think Mom is ready to take on the role of first lady of the United States right now." What Michael meant was that this would be a huge strain on our family life that I wasn't really ready to take on then. After much deliberation, once again trying not to "flap," but to listen to that still small voice, we made the decision to move back home to Indiana and run for governor. I finished out that school year, Michael was already in college, Charlotte was headed to college, and Audrey was finishing her junior year in high school.

When the time came to move back to Indiana for Mike to run for a higher office, I remember packing up the truck with all of our belongings and sitting on our front porch.

Mike looked at me and said, "Thank you."

"Thank you for what?" I asked.

He waved his arm, encompassing the whole street, and with tears in his eyes, answered, "Thank you for moving with me. I didn't miss all of this."

And off we went . . . again. Together.

CHAPTER SEVEN

Running for Governor

*Bees group together to keep the hive at a
consistent 93 degrees the entire year.*

When I was growing up, I never really considered moving away
from Indiana. But God had taken me to Washington, D.C.

As a congressional spouse, I had been stretched in ways I could
never have imagined. It had been hard work with many sacrifices.
It had some incredible highlights, too. But now God was calling us
back home to run for governor. While it was more comfortable for
us to be back in Indiana around our friends and family, it was still
a new environment—a new campaign on a larger level and a lot of
change for our family.

Columbus, Indiana, is unique. People come from all over the
world to see its varied architecture. J. Irwin Miller, of the Cummins
Engine Company in Columbus, worked hard to bring beautiful

architecture to the area in the 1950s. The downtown has quaint shops, delicious restaurants, and even an ice cream shop with a fully renovated pipe organ.

The first time I went to Columbus with Mike was when we were dating. I had my pilot's license, and Mike and I decided to fly down to Columbus from Indianapolis to take his dad, Ed, on an airplane ride. I remember having dinner with his family and then driving to Columbus Municipal Airport to take Ed for a tour of Columbus from the air. I really wanted to make a good impression on him.

Before taking off, a pilot has a checklist that they need to go through, step by step, in a specific order. Ed kept asking me a lot of questions and I got distracted from my checklist and skipped one step, the step where you turn on the outside lights. We took off and were having a delightful flight when the airport contacted me over the radio to alert me that my outside lights were not turned on. I quickly flipped the switch, but Ed never let me forget that moment, and made sure everyone in the family heard the story. There went my hopes for a good first impression.

Columbus was a special place for our family, and when Mike was done being vice president, Columbus Municipal Airport was where we would return for a final welcome-home rally, that same airport where I had tried to make a good first impression on Ed Pence.

While he was vice president, Mike had a practice of inviting guests aboard Air Force Two to ride in the cockpit on many of our trips. He always told them it gave them a unique "perspective," but he had never actually sat in the cockpit himself for a landing. On our final flight on Air Force Two, Mike rode in the cockpit and watched as that familiar heartland landscape came closer into view. After we landed, I introduced him for remarks to all of those gathered in Columbus on the tarmac. I told them that was the "perspective" he wanted to see as he came home.

We decided to announce Mike's gubernatorial campaign at the Columbus Commons, the downtown mall. The plan was for Audrey to introduce me, and I would introduce Mike. She had written her remarks on a napkin, and I wasn't sure what to expect, but she was poised, confident, and eloquent as always! We were all five there raising our clasped hands as the song "These Are My People" played on the loudspeaker. I enjoyed the governor campaign. It was great to be back in Indiana full-time and traveling all over our state. We had never campaigned statewide before. The campaign was centered around a "Roadmap for Indiana," and we traveled everywhere in a big red truck. Lots of Lincoln Day Dinners, sometimes together and sometimes solo. Most of these fall around Presidents' Day. But generally, they occur between January and May. With ninety-two counties, we had a lot of ground to cover. And we were still living in D.C., with me teaching school three days a week and Mike still serving in Congress.

Once we knew we won the primary in May 2012, we needed to move back home. That was a tough move.

Audrey had gone to school in Virginia since halfway through her kindergarten year, so moving back to Indiana meant she would be leaving all of her close friends, heading to a new school as a senior in high school. Senior year is a momentous time for everyone. This would be a huge sacrifice for Audrey to make. We still owned our home in Columbus, but we felt we needed to be centrally located for the campaign. We decided to let Audrey choose her school, and we would rent a house in that area while campaigning for governor. But it still wasn't easy. Audrey hadn't lived full time in Indiana for twelve years. She and I took a trip home to Indiana to visit several schools. She chose one that was very similar to the one she was currently attending in Virginia. Charlotte had started college at DePaul in Chicago, and Michael was at Purdue. It was nice to have everyone within driving distance again. We found a rental house, and yes, once again, we made the move. Our D.C. home had been much smaller, and I remember the cats racing around the house, not believing they had so much space! Being in Indiana allowed us to attend many more campaign events. Mike stayed with another congressman while he was in D.C. for votes.

There were lots of fairs, parades, and political events like chicken dinners. This campaign was not just in eleven counties like a congressional race, but ninety-two counties. We had to be very strategic to make sure we hit as many communities around the state as we could during the campaign.

There was great enthusiasm around the state for Mike's candidacy, and on November 6, 2012, Mike was elected as the fiftieth governor of Indiana. Our watch party where we waited for the returns was held in Lucas Oil Stadium, the home of the Colts. We were graciously allowed by the Lucas family to use their suite for our family and close friends.

The evening was wearing on as the final results came late. That night, my kids all had a present for Mike. And right after we found out we had won, it was time to head down to the stage. Supporters were waiting. And it was late. But we wanted a moment just the five of us . . . a moment to hold on to each other before the roller coaster headed down the slope. The kids wanted to give Mike their gifts. We are a family that tries to mark special occasions with gifts or mementos. So, we huddled . . . in the bathroom . . . because it was the only privacy we could find. It was very tender. After giving

Mike his gifts, I was surprised to learn that my kids had a gift for me. It is probably the best gift I have ever received. My kids gave me a three-section silver frame. In each section they each wrote their favorite "momism."

Michael wrote, "I'm not going to let what's going on out there affect what's going on in here." This had been my mantra from early on. Politics can be a messy place, and our family life was sacred to me. Criticism as well as praise could really have done a number on our family life if I had let it intrude into our private space. I decided early on that I was not going to let all of the "muck" that is part of a political life affect all of the amazing things that were going on in our family life. Mike consistently put his BlackBerry in a little dish right on the piano by the front door every evening when he came home. Being a member of Congress requires a huge time commitment, but once he was home for the evening, he tried to focus exclusively on me and the kids.

Charlotte's momism was "You teach your kids how to fight for their dreams by fighting for yours." Our kids had seen us make the sacrifices necessary to become successful in politics. They knew the stories of the two past failed campaigns. They had heard about the lessons learned and how we didn't let failure or fear stop us from trying again. We raised them to search for the gifts and strengths God had given each of them. We taught them to think for themselves. They watched us daily make the sacrifices to serve.

Audrey's was "I hear you, and I'm listening. Greatest words I could ever hear." With all the struggles that come with being a political family, probably the hardest was having to move Audrey in her senior year in high school. Audrey competed in We the People, an organization for high school students to debate topics, relying on the foundation of principles in the Constitution. I always find it fascinating when life experiences come full circle.

Audrey would go on to graduate from Yale Law School and become a lawyer.

During her first semester at the new high school in Indiana, at a particularly difficult time, I had spoken those words of the "momism" to her. I was sitting on a bench on Capitol Hill, having traveled back to D.C. for a few meetings. She was struggling with the adjustment to a new school, and a new environment. She missed her friends, her life in D.C., and her school, and she called me during the school day. I thanked God that she called me, that she wanted to talk to her mom. I thank God that I knew at that moment that I needed to be completely present and completely supportive of her struggle. This was not a time to tell her to "suck it up." This was a time to let her know I got it. I understood. I empathized. So I said, "I hear you, and I'm listening."

What I have learned about parenting is that it really doesn't wait until I have time to sit down and collect my thoughts. Life happens all the time, not just at convenient times, and I learned to stop and pray before handling a sticky situation. I learned to rely on my faith, my friends, and to read everything I could about how to parent any particular age. Just like Mike's dad had told us when we were trying to have children, kids aren't born as teenagers. So you do have time to prepare for parenting that age and I tried to remember that as our kids grew.

Election night was a great evening, and once again, the five of us held our hands clasped in the air in victory, just like we had at the announcement months earlier. Mike would not be sworn in as governor until January, as he was still completing his term as congressman. So we stayed in our rental house in Indiana until we could move into the Governor's Residence. November 6 was when some of our security detail started for the first time. Suddenly, cameras were being installed around the rental home. During my years as first lady and second lady, the lack of privacy was the most difficult part. But having a security detail as first lady was an adjustment that helped prepare me for my time as second lady, where I had a lot more security around me. Once again, looking back, I could see God's hand in all of this.

That Christmas we had planned to go to San Antonio for a family vacation, but a huge snowstorm hit, and our flights were canceled. So we decided to just get in the car and drive up to Michigan and ski. Michael was helping Charlotte learn to snowboard that year. They stayed out on the slopes for hours, even though it was bitterly cold. Audrey and I were not interested in skiing much under those conditions. It was just the four of us because Mike had been called back to Washington for votes before we had even left for Michigan, and he was even voting on New Year's Eve, as the rest of us celebrated in Michigan. We called him on New Year's Eve at midnight in another odd family memory. He finally made it to Michigan on New Year's Day.

And so the governor years for our family began.

CHAPTER EIGHT

Moving to the Governor's Residence

*Bees use a sticky material called propolis, taken
from the buds of trees, to fill in cracks of their
hives and make them weatherproof.*

When I became first lady, one of the first things I did was to meet
with all of the former first ladies of Indiana to get their advice.
Proverbs 11:14 says, "For lack of guidance a nation falls, but victory is won through many advisers." I wanted to know everything
they wanted to share with me. Their tips were invaluable. What I
learned from them was that I could be "me" in this new role.

There is so little time to prepare for this role, and it helped
me so much to realize I could learn from these ladies' wisdom
without feeling like I had to reinvent the wheel. And they were
very gracious to share. I remember the late Susan Bayh meeting me for lunch in downtown Indy. She suggested that I write
three to four speeches that I could change slightly for the venue

where I was speaking. She said that I would be too busy to draft a specific speech every time I would be asked to give remarks. Judy O'Bannon invited me to her lovely home, not far from the Governor's Residence. She shared with me how she had invited local students and artists to the Residence as she hung varied local artwork throughout the home on a rotating schedule. Maggie Kernan and I spoke by phone, and Cheri Daniels invited me to the Residence before Mike was even sworn in and gave me the tour of the home, and then we sat for a while and chatted in her personal office upstairs. She had furnished it with a beautiful desk and a flowered couch that I moved to my office at the Statehouse once I became the first lady.

After the holidays, we once again packed up, moved out of our rental home and got settled in the Governor's Residence. (In Indiana, it is called the Residence, not the Mansion.) It was close enough for Audrey to drive to school each morning.

The Governor's Residence is a beautiful Tudor home on six acres, and we were the first family to live there full-time in eight years. It's the second-smallest governor's residence in the country, and the family living space is located on the second and third floors above the official public area. The yard is spacious with beautiful vegetable and flower gardens and mature trees lining the road. We had a wonderful groundskeeper who always used to tease me about walking barefoot outside. I guess he was surprised to find the first lady without shoes on. He did an amazing job taking care of the bulk of the property. But the planting of annuals each spring fell to the Marion County Master Gardener volunteers. They worked tirelessly to make the Governor's Residence beautiful. Weekly, they would sign up for specific times to come tend to the gardens. I remember treating them to lunch one hot spring day after their work was completed!

The governor and first lady are stewards of the home. And we took that role seriously. We wanted Hoosiers to be proud of the care we took to preserve this special place. We made a lot of improvements to the home, including adding extensive patio furniture to a large, brick patio where we, along with future governors and their spouses, could host events. I think our first event held on that patio was a Pacers party when the Pacers were in the playoffs. We are big Indiana sports fans.

Trying to maintain some sense of normalcy, we also added wooden double doors at the top of the winding stairs that could be locked in the evening and kept closed when we wanted privacy. We did allow tours of the main floor on Thursdays, so we needed a way to keep our pets corralled during those tours and during official events at the house. Otherwise, anyone in the home could just meander upstairs. Going up the back stairs to the personal residential area, the home was set up so that we had to walk down a long hallway or go through Charlotte's bedroom to get to the kitchen and family room, so we cut a hole in the wall to install a door. It made the rooms flow more smoothly and gave Charlotte some privacy.

When I think of the Governor's Residence, I don't think first about the large mansion or the countless events that we held there. The memories that come to mind are how many times we had to chase our beagle, Maverick, up and down the busy street where the mansion is located. While I did raise private funds to have two gates installed at each drive's entrance, there is no fence around the perimeter of the property. Beagles are hounds. Once they have a scent, they follow it anywhere. Maverick amazingly survived his few escapes, only to pass away of old age during the 2016 presidential campaign. The home doesn't have a chef, and no one is in the house after business hours. During the weekdays, there is the housekeeper, Candee Hopkins, and the butler. Dexter Powell recently retired from that position after over thirty years of service. There is also a guard shack right by the entrance to the home.

We had a lot of fond memories at the Residence. We celebrated Audrey's graduation from high school there. And it was there that our son told us he was going to ask Sarah to marry him. We have prayed for our children's future spouses ever since they were born. The minute he and Sarah called us to tell us the news, I was filled with this amazing love for Sarah. We had Sarah's bridal shower there. She and Michael even had a small intimate wedding at the house right before we moved out.

Like any home, there was always something in need of repair or updating. We really wanted to keep the house in great condition and improve where we could. There was a huge flagpole that we had been told was beginning to lean to one side. It was hidden among some towering evergreens, and wasn't really even visible from the street. We were being encouraged to find a spot for a new flagpole. Well, Mike needed very little encouragement to begin planning a new spot for a new one. (When we moved back to Indiana after the 2020 election, the first thing he ordered for our new home was his flagpole.) So, after much planning, on June 4, 2014, he and I joined members of the American Legion to unveil and dedicate the Veterans Flagstaff Memorial Marker at the Governor's Residence. We also placed the Indiana seal on the brick wall behind the flagpole so that visitors who come for a photo would have something marking the photo as being taken at the Governor's Residence. Of all of the improvements we made to that residence, I think the flagpole is the thing Mike is most proud of!

There is a small garden that sits on the corner of Forty-Sixth Street and Meridian Street in front of the Governor's Residence. It was overgrown, received little water since it was situated very far from the house, and was in dire need of a facelift. I invited Purdue agriculture students to design a garden for that corner. They had so many great ideas, and incorporated native perennial plants. They truly designed a beautiful garden and the Purdue Extension–Marion County Master Gardeners planted the Centennial Garden on the grounds of the Governor's Residence in the summer of 2014. Every time I drive by, I look to see how it is faring! We all celebrated with a lunch on the patio after it was completed.

Indiana's bicentennial was coming up in 2016, so we re-upholstered the existing furniture in the formal living room in blues and golds in our second year to celebrate our state's colors. The Governor's Residence Foundation committee designed some beautiful china incorporating elements of our state flag. It was gorgeous. This dedicated group of women also helped immensely with Christmas decoration themes and budgets. They were amazing and helped so much.

I wanted to use this time to bless other people, and those who had served before us and helped me figure out what my role would be. The house had several place settings from Evan and Susan Bayh's china. We wanted to add a set of china to commemorate our state's bicentennial. Private funds were raised for any expenses incurred by the Residence Foundation. When Frank and Judy O'Bannon had been governor and first lady, tragically Frank died suddenly while in office. They weren't living at the Residence at the time due to construction work going on; Judy had spearheaded a much-needed renovation to include a large community room, office, and catering kitchen. The Indiana guild of the World Organization of China Painters had offered to gift to Judy and the Residence an entire set of hand-painted china, illustrating Indiana's wildflowers. She had not been serving as first lady when the set was completed. So one of the first things I did as first lady was to invite the painters and Judy to a luncheon where she could have the opportunity to thank them, and they could enjoy a lunch served on their dishes at the Governor's Residence. It was a special afternoon.

The Residence was a great place to live, but it was still important for us to get some time away together as a family where we could rest and recuperate. One of our favorite places to go during Mike's time as governor was the Aynes House cabin in Brown County State Park, which is the governor's retreat in Indiana. It has a beautiful overlook of Indiana's rolling hills. It was a place for us to get away and truly relax. Our kids loved going there as well. Even though it was just an hour from the Statehouse, we felt like we were a thousand miles away. We could hike, sit on the screened-in porch, grill out on the deck, and ride our bikes all over the park. It was a place to truly refresh.

Views from the park were painted extensively by T. C. Steele, a famous Indiana landscape artist. In fact, Mike hung a T. C. Steele painting depicting a scenic overlook of this landscape in his White House vice president's office and another in his ceremonial office in the Senate.

Aynes House is named after the family who constructed it. It can be dated back to the late 1920s or early 1930s. The house had seen better days and hadn't been updated in some time. As first lady, I was approached by the head of the Indiana Department of Natural Resources to see if we might be interested in overseeing some renovations. The Indiana Governor's Residence Foundation is permitted to raise private money for just such a purpose. The amazing women on that board dug in and really worked hard to get the job done. Many supporters donated time and materials to do the actual work. The house was also furnished by another wonderful supporter. We spent our first Thanksgiving there and many holidays and weekends that followed. We held staff meetings and retreats there. The Brown County staff are truly amazing, and always welcomed us with open arms.

Eric and Janet Holcomb, who followed us as governor and first lady, graciously allowed us to visit the cabin for several weekends while Mike was vice president. We didn't own the Indiana home we had during his time in Congress anymore. We had sold it when Mike became governor, so we didn't really have a home to come back to for holidays. His first year as vice president, we spent Christmas at Aynes House. We walked in and were greeted by the park staff. They had a fire roaring, the song "Back Home in Indiana" playing, and the Christmas tree decorated all in red, with little cardinal ornaments all over it. The cardinal is Indiana's state bird. We were choked up, to say the least. Because the Secret Service could stay overnight right there in the park at the public cabins and the lodge, Aynes House was an easy place for them to protect us.

While being a good steward of everything related to the Residence and Aynes House required a huge commitment, I felt like it was my job, and my duty, really. I hadn't anticipated how much of my time would be required to maintain the homes, but this was part of the responsibility as first lady. And it was where God had placed me for that season.

There were some roles that I wasn't expecting. As I settled into this new position, it was hard for me to believe that Christmas decorating—whether it be the Governor's Residence, the Indiana Statehouse, or later at the Vice President's Residence—officially fell to me. Decorating these beautiful spaces was a big job. Suddenly, Christmas decorating was not only part of family time, but now it was my job—and a big endeavor.

I gathered the members of the Residence Foundation committee to talk through decorations for the house. We quickly realized that professionally lighting trees all over the property was cost prohibitive. So the members of the committee, dear friends who gave a lot of time to improve the Governor's Residence as well as Aynes House, came up with several ideas for decorating. We incorporated ornaments from counties all over the state on the tree in the entry foyer and decided on a Hoosier theme using cardinals. We were able to decorate the home very tastefully, hang wreaths outside, and light a large artificial tree with multicolored lights—Mike's favorite—in the gazebo in the front yard. Everything looked beautiful!

In my first year, when I hadn't yet realized that decorating the Statehouse for Christmas was a task that fell to me, the end result was less than desirable. The tradition had been to let fourth graders from around the state create their own ornaments and bring them in, but not fully understanding my role, we hadn't really coordinated with teachers in advance, and so the decorations ended up being quickly colored paper ornaments hung on one lone tree with no lights or garland of any kind. I received a lot of complaints about the decorations that first year.

But I learned from it . . .
Right now, this was my role.

The second year, I decided to go all out. Not only did I take on decorating the Statehouse with gusto, I also had events at the Statehouse where I invited students from all over the state to come see the tree lighting there. Each grade from kindergarten to fifth had their own tree with its own theme. I used my art teacher experience and set up stations all around the main floor of the Statehouse and had fun ornaments for each student to create and take home. I had enlisted the help of retired teacher friends. We had reindeer made from pipe cleaners, clear glass globes the students painted to create snowmen and Santa faces, and old-fashioned Christmas trees made from fabric and small sticks from the Governor's Residence. My friend Kathy Riley loves to decorate for Christmas, so I put her in charge of decorating each tree. One was even a Grinch tree, and Kathy dressed up as the Grinch! Each grade level had one student push the button to light their tree. In my last year as first lady, one large tree was decorated for the 2016 bicentennial with lots of historical ornaments. It was spectacular. This was my last opportunity to decorate the Statehouse, and I felt a real sense of accomplishment being able to celebrate with students from around the state and to highlight our bicentennial.

We also started a tree-lighting ceremony the first year in the Governor's Residence, inviting local schoolchildren to the house on December 1 to light the official tree. Mike would read from our family's copy of "The Night Before Christmas," by Clement C. Moore, which Mike's mom gave him when we had our first child. And I would read the Christmas story from Luke, chapter 2, in the

Bible. We would have snacks and activities for the kids, and it was a good way for me to use the knowledge I'd gained from all of those playgroups with the kids and days of teaching. I remember our beagle, Maverick, somehow getting downstairs and trying to eat cookies out of the children's hands! The second year we decided to do the Christmas theme in blues and golds to go with the furniture in the official living room that we had re-covered in Indiana's colors. We recycled decorations from year to year while trying to change things up a bit. Each year, the Indiana Christmas Tree Growers Association donated two Christmas trees to the Residence.

Decorating at Christmas for us, as it is for many people, has always been a way to truly feel home during the holidays. We usually decorated our Indiana home after a long drive back home after December votes were over and school was out. One year when Mike was in Congress, we pulled into the driveway and unloaded the car, and Mike and I decided to head out to pick up some groceries. It was then that we became aware that our minivan had no reverse function. This was pretty discouraging after a long drive home. Mike and I realized we needed to take it in for repair immediately. So we put it in neutral and it rolled down our driveway. We headed to the dealership, where we were told there was no way to fix it. We looked at the few used vans on their lot, bought one, and headed to get takeout for our dinner. We were so tired when we turned into our street, and we knew the kids would want us to start decorating. But honestly, that is the last thing in the world we wanted to do. Little did we know that Michael had assembled our girls and they all had worked very hard to decorate our house for

Christmas. When we pulled into our street, our house was lit up with lights on the bushes, our wreath on the door, candles in the window, and tons of decorations. We were completely surprised and both started crying. It was a moving moment and truly a blessing from our amazing kids. This was the best Christmas present!

What God was teaching me through the many experiences of being first lady was that, while many of my responsibilities weren't exactly glamorous, He was using me to touch the lives of a lot of Hoosiers and using me to be a good caretaker of the places where He took us. Sometimes, that meant filling in the cracks and taking great care of the Governor's Residence and Aynes House.

CHAPTER NINE

First Lady of Indiana

*A worker bee can move a load of nectar or pollen that
is the same as 80 percent of her own body weight.*

There are two types of leadership. The first type is the world's idea
of leading. All too often, when we step into leadership roles we do
so looking for the spotlight, or seeking to elevate ourselves. God's
idea of leadership is much different, focused instead on being a servant and a steward of the gifts we've been given. I tried to keep
that definition of leadership in mind as I took on a position of far
greater scope than I'd ever faced. In leaning into that role, I found
that I had skills I didn't know I'd been building, learned to rely on
a group of wise friends, and found the secret of being present and
engaged where you are.

With each election cycle, once the new governors-elect are
decided, the Republican and Democratic governors' associations

hold a retreat to help the new governors-to-be prepare for their time of service. There are several sessions devoted to the spouses as well. These were especially helpful to me. For some reason, it had never even crossed my mind that I would need to begin planning for Mike's inauguration. But at a small luncheon during this retreat, all of the spouses began sharing thoughts and suggestions for our inauguration since they had been down this road before. They also gave me great advice regarding my initiative. They said not to rush into anything, but to carefully evaluate the opportunities that would be presented to me.

I headed home from that retreat and started plans with a gusto. The woman who had made my wedding dress offered to make my gown for the ball. I quickly agreed! That dress is still one of my favorites. Meanwhile, Mike was busy conducting interviews for his cabinet and planning his agenda. It was a super-busy time. Plus, we were packing up getting ready to move . . . again!

The actual inauguration was held outside in freezing weather. We had hot chocolate stands and hand warmers for those in attendance. Afterward, everyone quickly came inside the Statehouse for an informal reception. That same evening was the Inaugural Ball. The food at the ball was down-home good Hoosier fare, the band was super fun, and everyone seemed to have a good time! We had a multidenominational faith ceremony the day after Mike's swearing-in. Inauguration and all that went with it came and went, we moved into the Residence, and my life as first lady began.

I once asked my first lady staff to tell me what stood out in their minds from our years at the Statehouse. My deputy chief of staff said she would never forget the first meeting Mike had as governor with the entire staff. He talked to them about servant leadership. We had been given an amazing opportunity to serve the people of Indiana, and Mike and I wanted to use this opportunity to inspire our staff to step up to the task. Right now, in this moment, it was our turn, my turn as first lady of Indiana to really impact the lives of my fellow Hoosiers for the better.

I wanted to be a good steward of the position into which God had placed me. This was a message I wanted Hoosiers and my family and friends to take away from my time of service. I wanted to wear the mantle and be available for whatever God might call me to as first lady. I wanted to honor Him.

We all face challenges and opportunities in our own lives. We are asked to help with a situation or lead a project or respond to a need. My suggestion to the reader is to look at those moments and think through whether this is something you should tackle. When my kids were toddlers, I was attending a Bible study, and the lead teacher suggested I begin leading a small group. At that time, I really did not feel called to take on that huge responsibility. I told her that Mike and I would pray about it, though. Neither one of us thought it would be a good idea, so I called her back and graciously declined. At that time, my ministry was Michael, Charlotte, and Audrey. Sometimes God isn't calling us to a certain ministry. And sometimes it takes a lot of prayer and discussion to discern if it's the right thing or not. We can't say yes to every opportunity.

There are always so many needs, and so going forward with new possibilities as first lady, I wanted to be sensitive to what I could and couldn't accomplish. I used to tell people that I wanted to take advantage of the fact that people were more eager to take my phone calls during this period of time. My season as first lady would give me a foundation heading into the years I would spend as second lady, although I didn't know it at the time.

I wanted to be very active as first lady. Colossians 3:23a says, "Whatever you do, work at it with all your heart, as working for the Lord . . ." Again . . . I felt that if this was where God put me, then this was where I would try to shine. While there was a small office at the Governor's Residence for staff, I chose to have my official office at the Statehouse. This allowed for meetings to be held there, opportunities for students from all over the state to visit, and a place from which to coordinate many of the initiatives I championed as first lady. We made sure the office was super inviting, with coffee and a comfy couch always available. By the time I left four years later, the walls were covered with artwork from art therapy and children from around the state.

I quickly hired my small three-person staff: a chief of staff, deputy chief of staff who was also the Residence manager, and personal aide. At the very first official staff meeting, I began to feel a lot of pain in my upper abdomen. I assumed it was due to my lunch. I leaned back on the couch in the office to see if it felt any better. My deputy chief of staff said it could be my gallbladder. As the pain intensified, I decided to head home with my state trooper. Halfway home, I told him to just take me to the hospital. Once there, the first thing they did was make sure I wasn't having a heart attack. I called Mike, but Audrey's school was close by, so she hurried over to be with me. The doctor quickly realized I needed to have my gallbladder removed. He sent me home with pain medicine for the night, and my gallbladder was removed the following morning. It's quite an experience to have your gallbladder surgery on the evening news! Two weeks later, we went to a neighborhood party where a gallbladder specialist thanked me for his new notoriety!

Back in the office again, we began to make plans. Being first lady meant many groups reached out to persuade me to champion their cause. I was being inundated with requests. Not only are there many official duties like riding in the Indy 500 Festival Parade and dyeing the downtown canal green on St. Patrick's Day, but we needed to decide where to give the surplus private funds raised for our inaugural celebration. My first official act as first lady was presenting a check for the remaining $100,000 to the Indiana National Guard Relief Fund on February 8, 2013, which was very exciting and special. This fund is used for families who may need a little help with unexpected financial hardships that may occur while a service member is deployed. This was a great way to start my four years, helping our amazing Indiana National Guard families.

Mike and I eagerly participated in as many events and activities as we could, from Mike throwing out the first pitch for an Indianapolis Indians game to walking in the Walk for MS with our friend Jamie Broyles, to walking the Indy 500 Festival Mini-Marathon 5K. And it was during my first year as first lady that I learned how to milk a cow! We enjoyed hosting events at the Residence, including a cookout with all of the Indiana delegation and their families. Having served in Congress, we realized how hard the members and their families work, and we wanted to show them how much we appreciated them. In 2014, I hosted the 2014 Arts for All Fest at the Governor's Residence, which gives students the opportunity to explore the visual arts, drama, music, and movement. Approximately three hundred students with disabilities were in attendance. It was raining all day, but we were undaunted. We had large tents set up all over the lawn, and everyone had a blast.

We also tried to keep traditions going that had been in place. Halloween was a main event at the Governor's Residence, and it had been a tradition for years for the governor and first lady to dress up and pass out candy.

The first year, Halloween was delayed due to rain, so we had an indoor party with some local schoolchildren on Halloween, then the next night we passed out candy and asked the mascot for the Pacers to attend. Mike wore an Andrew Luck jersey, and I was dressed as a Fever player. The next year we asked Garfield the Cat and creator Jim Davis to join us. I was a honeybee and Mike was a beekeeper. In 2015, Mike was a cowboy and I was a "first" lady bug. In 2016, I had planned to wear a costume that would be reminiscent of Indiana's early days in honor of our bicentennial. But our plans were interrupted when we suddenly found ourselves on the national ticket. Since we were on the campaign trail on October 31, I had a member of my staff dress up in the outfit and distribute candy as planned. We couldn't let the tradition wane.

That first spring, I also visited lots of schools all over the state, from public to charter to private. That was one of my favorite things to do because not only did I get to be with students, which I absolutely love, but I also was able to encourage educators. They are amazing!

In August 2013, I visited Glen Acres Elementary School in Lafayette to kick off an art exchange between third-grade students in Lafayette and its Japanese sister city, Ota City. This was such a treat to be back in the classroom teaching art. I decided it would be a great way to share what the kids look like by doing a self-portrait where the students draw themselves wearing mirror sunglasses with the reflection being their favorite activity or being in their favorite place. That way they would not only be sharing with the Japanese children a picture of themselves, but they would be revealing an important aspect of who they were. Some drew sporting events, others Disney World, and some beach vacations.

We traveled to Japan in September, and I shared the self-portraits drawn by Lafayette students with the students at Ota Elementary School. The children in Japan loved them. Then I taught the Japanese students how to do the exact same project, and I took their portraits home with me to share with the Lafayette students. It was such a successful exchange as part of Sister Cities International. Their mission is to promote peace through mutual respect, understanding, and cooperation—one individual, one community at a time.

I completed the art project with the Japanese students with Charlotte's help since she was able to join me on this trip to Japan. Afterward, I went to visit some of the other classrooms, wearing my Japanese slippers that we were given to wear upon arrival. As I entered one classroom, they recited some prose for me. I reciprocated by singing a Japanese song for them that my sister had taught me when she was an exchange student years before in Ota City. It is a very popular song in Japan called "Sukiyaki." Once I started singing, the students all joined in. It was a super fun, spontaneous moment. I think I shocked my staff in the process! That evening we had a reception where my staff encouraged me to sing it for the adults, and sure enough, the moment I started singing, the entire group joined in.

There were many more opportunities to work with students and share our Indiana culture with people in other countries. In March 2014, I visited with 115 fourth graders at Parkside Elementary School in Columbus, Indiana. The students there had designed a banner for me to take to Germany and present to Columbus' sister city, Lohne. That trip was so enjoyable because the people of Lohne shared so many stories with me about their favorite experiences in Columbus. It truly was remarkable how that brought us together. I couldn't get enough of hearing about their favorite ice cream shop in Indiana or their experiences with Hoosier families who had hosted them. They were sharing with me their memories about places near and dear to my heart. While in Germany, we watched a live feed of the Indiana Pacers game against the Oklahoma City Thunder. I was also able to do an art sculpture replica exchange between the Indianapolis Museum of Art and the Museum Ludwig, located in Cologne, Germany, Indianapolis' sister city. I toured the Berlin-Weissensee School of Art's art therapy program, where I heard about their fascinating experiences using art therapy with a blind young man.

Mike and I enjoyed hosting the Governor's Arts Awards and I tried to get to the current exhibit at the Indianapolis Museum of Art as frequently as I could. Another very exciting cultural event that Indianapolis hosts every four years is the International Violin Competition of Indianapolis, for young violinists from all over the world. It is truly extraordinary! I also had the honor of keynoting their Juried Exhibition of Student Art Awards, held at Hilbert Circle Theatre downtown.

Once again, God had been preparing me for this in the past, but I had no idea He was doing so at the time. My love of art and watercolor painting helped me to relate to these young people. I knew what it felt like to be respected as an artist and to use God's gift for His glory through art and creativity.

I shared a story with the young people there about how my sister-in-law, Kim, had once given me a charm as a gift. I was wearing it on a silver chain around my neck as I addressed these young artists. I showed them that it was a charm of a painter's palette. It had meant so much to me because it meant Kim saw me as an artist. And I told them that day, as they competed in the exclusive juried art exhibit, I, and all of those present, saw each of them as an artist. Their artwork was exquisite. They gifted me with a set of notecards showcasing these incredible pieces of artwork that all featured violins in some way. I still have them, and I only use them for very special notes.

As first lady, I wanted to make a difference, but some of the lessons I passed on were things God had been teaching me my whole life. I was asked to speak to America's Best Hope. This is a Christian organization that was holding a conference in Indianapolis.

This was probably my favorite speech that I ever gave. It was titled "Who's on Your Stool?" and began:

One of my favorite moments in an ordinary day is when I am preparing dinner (yes . . . I still prepare dinner . . . there is no cook at the Governor's Residence). Anyway, I love it when I'm putzing around the kitchen, cutting vegetables, maybe putting some water on to boil, sautéing something . . . and one of my kids is sitting on the stool. [I had a counter stool with me that I had brought from home.] It's really a special moment. Because it usually means we are engaged. They are talking . . . I am listening . . . or I am talking and they are listening. It's almost magical. I love it. Because in those moments, I'm not staring them in the eye. I'm just present. They seem to be more free to talk. They can unburden themselves. And they have Mom's full attention . . . but it just seems to be easier to talk to Mom when I'm putzing. And in those moments wisdom is imparted. In those moments, God uses me. In those moments problems get solved, life gets a little easier. The load is shared.

Sometimes those moments occur in the car. It's the same dynamic. Mom is focused on driving, but there is an opportunity to maybe share a problem or concern without feeling too exposed. The focus is turned outside the car . . . and in those moments my kids seem to be able to share . . . hey, Mom . . . by the way, I was thinking . . . Those moments in my life have come sometimes without warning . . . sometimes without me having a chance to research what I was going to say . . . sometimes those moments come on a wing and a prayer. . . .

After I finished the entire speech, challenging the listeners to be aware of opportunities right in front of them to make a difference in someone's life, my staff met me backstage. They were very emotional, and I realized I had touched a nerve for them. A few weeks later, my chief of staff resigned, telling me she had been convinced by my remarks to go back home to Fort Wayne, Indiana, to invest in a relationship with a man who wanted to marry her. They did end up marrying, and now are very happy! It was a good reminder to me that relationships are more important than accomplishments. God was placing me in a position to really invest in people's lives—even the lives of people around me. It was a humbling realization, and I wanted to be sure to protect against getting caught up in the momentum of the office.

We have to invest in the relationships with the people who are on our "stool," and I tried to do that as often as I could—with my kids, my staff, and the people God placed in my path. Our relationship with Jesus is also like that. It's a relationship, a friendship, and this realization that I can have a personal relationship with Jesus, one that I had started to understand so many years ago when I was dating Mike, only grew with time.

Being first lady also opened up so many opportunities to come alongside wonderful Hoosiers and Indiana organizations. I tried to be a support to as many groups as I could that worked to strengthen families, support the arts, and help our servicemen and -women. There were so many that, as I look back over my time as first lady, I smile at all of the exceptional organizations that exist.

But I couldn't say yes to everyone, and I wanted to help bring awareness and resources to as many of these incredible groups as I could. I needed a creative solution.

A friend of mine who had been very involved in the Washington, D.C., First Lady's Luncheon, Patti Coons, kept approaching me with the suggestion that I host my own First Lady's Luncheon.

I kept thinking, *I can't give a luncheon in my own honor! And how would I pay for it?* But eventually, things began to click in my brain. I realized that if I started a charitable foundation, I could raise funds to support causes and charities around the state . . . Then, when any supporters of the myriad of causes contacted me, I could suggest they apply for a grant from my foundation. Our lawyer helped me set up the Indiana First Lady's Charitable Foundation, and I asked five close friends from all over the state to serve on its board. Our mission was to reward charities that supported youth and families. We created a rubric for evaluating each and every applicant. I started working with an amazing event planner to plan the inaugural Indiana First Lady's Luncheon.

The first luncheon featured custom bags created by Indiana-based Vera Bradley for each attendee. The tablecloths were also custom created by them. Our theme was "Helping Indiana's Children Bloom." We focused on art therapy and awarded a check for $100,000 to Riley Hospital for Children's Art Therapy Initiative. Our special performer was Indiana's own Sandi Patty. We invited all former Indiana first ladies. Each table had a custom-painted centerpiece bowl with peonies painted on them by the Indiana chapter of the World Organization of China Painters. I did a watercolor of the state flower, the peony, and we included a print in each attendee's gift bag. Over the course of the year, we awarded quarterly grants of $500 or $1,000 to charities all over the state. We invited the recipients to a breakfast at the Governor's Residence where we presented them with their check, a picture, and a generic press release for them to take back to their respective communities to hopefully garner some hometown support. At the first quarterly awards ceremony, twenty-eight charities were awarded grants totaling $22,000. It was a humbling experience for me every time we awarded grants.

The second year of the First Lady's Charitable Foundation luncheon, we focused on Hoosier Homegrown as our theme. The entertainer was Josh Kaufman, our very own Hoosier winner of the television show *The Voice*. The custom centerpieces were custom-woven baskets, made by Hoosier basket weavers from Barnyard Baskets. The gift bags at each place setting were oilcloth custom bags by the Farmer's Wife, and everyone received a first lady's cookbook, an Indiana-shaped cutting board, seed packets, and honey from the Governor's Residence beehive, and a print of my painting of the iconic Indiana Ball jar with wildflowers. Our large check went to Feeding Indiana's Hungry. In planning that luncheon, we learned so much about food insecurity right here in our own state. This was a huge opportunity to bring awareness to this issue.

So many Hoosiers have taken a tragedy or heartbreak and turned it into something to help others going through the same heartache. It was inspiring. Instead of focusing on the difficulties of their situations, these people were focusing on the positive. You know, we all have trials, every single one of us. And sometimes they can be debilitating. But I took strength from hearing the stories of these amazing Hoosiers and seeing how they used difficult situations to help others.

Being first lady brought some other inspiring experiences where I saw how people came alongside one another in challenging situations.

I joined the ladies of Indy SurviveOars, Indiana's only breast cancer dragon boat team, at their team practice at Geist Reservoir. I offered remarks to the women and presented each woman with a Vera Bradley–designed bag in honor of their fight and courage. The pink bags were the very same ones designed and donated by

Vera Bradley for the inaugural First Lady's Luncheon held in April to support the Indiana First Lady's Charitable Foundation. The enthusiasm these women exhibited was contagious. After breast surgery, one of the best things a woman can do is to exercise the upper body. These women turned that into something fun. To see them racing this big pink dragon boat through the reservoir was such an example of resilience. I must say, as I rowed alongside them as a guest rower that day at practice, I was probably the one with the least amount of arm strength.

While being first lady allowed me to have new learning experiences and to grow from them, it also meant that some traditions for me had to change.

In 2014, I remember vividly attending Penrod Arts Fair at the Indianapolis Museum of Art. Penrod is held every September. It is the most beautiful art fair, with a huge variety of art available for purchase. In the early 1990s, I was fortunate enough to be juried into the fair. I set up my booth the night before with as many watercolors as I could complete before the show.

Painting was an opportunity for me to do something creative in the midst of being a mom of three young children. I first took watercolor classes when my eldest, Michael, was a baby. Monday nights were my chance to go do something for me, so Mike was in charge of Michael on those nights. It was good for me, and it was good for both of them.

As the years went by and we had two more children, I painted during nap time, and I was as busy as I could be preparing for exhibitions. The first year I exhibited in Penrod, I barely sold anything. Even though many of the customers admired my paintings, unless they had a need for a "barn," or a "magnolia blossom," or a "pot of geraniums," I wasn't going to be able to sell anything. About that same time, family members noticed my watercolors and started asking me to do watercolors of their homes. It was then that I started my online business, Custom Home Watercolors. I decided to make a color copy of each home that I painted so that I could mat the copies and display them in my booth the next year at Penrod. It made much more sense to me to take custom orders at the fair, because then I knew the time and effort I was putting into a watercolor would result in income.

I was blessed to have been admitted into Penrod several years where I sold my custom home watercolors. It was always one of my favorite days of the year. I loved going the night before to set up my tent and then arriving early in the morning while the mist was rising off the grass at the museum grounds with the sun peeking through the trees. I would always head to the coffee and donut tent and grab some early morning sustenance—coffee and donuts—before the gates opened. It was just so much fun chatting with all of the other artists and helping each other out, setting up our booths and getting each other coffee. I always ended up buying something special to remember each fair. Mike would come some time during the day and bring the kids and watch my booth while I went to get lunch. He sold a painting or two while he was there.

Having moved so many times myself, I understood what a home can mean no matter how long one lives there. There is something about a watercolor of your home. I loved being able to paint a family memento for my clients. Some of the homes were beautiful, extravagant places with lush landscaping. I used to say I added Miracle-Gro to the paint when I painted the landscaping. Some paintings were done from a single photograph of a home that maybe was long gone by then, but was a memory that someone wanted preserved. One was of a home that had burned. One was for a woman who wanted me to paint the home her mother had lived in for decades to be able to hang it in her mom's room in her senior care facility. After I started doing custom home watercolors, I painted most of the homes we ourselves had lived in. They fill an entire wall in our home now.

As first lady, I no longer had a booth, but I went to the fair and did interviews promoting Penrod. It was strange being a visitor instead of an exhibitor, but it was one of the ways I was able to continue my love of art while being in this new role.

During my last year as first lady, the Indiana State Fair honored me with an exhibit devoted to my watercolors. We printed replicas of many of my paintings, framed them, and hauled them out to the Home and Family Arts Building. This was especially moving to me, because for many years before Mike was a congressman, I would enter a watercolor into the competition. My first watercolor I ever entered received a third-place ribbon. It was a painting of a white rocker on a white porch with a little table holding a book with a grassy field in the distance. I have that painting hanging in my home to this day with the faded pink ribbon taped to the back.

Some of the opportunities as first lady were easier to implement than others. Having a small staff and budget, we looked for those projects to promote. One was Hopeline, sponsored by Verizon. It simply involved setting out boxes at strategic locations in the Indiana Statehouse and asking for donations of old phones that could be donated for use by victims of domestic violence. Sometimes,

God is just asking us to be aware of our position to be able to help someone else, whatever that position may be.

Another easy issue to promote was bringing awareness to the issue of infant mortality in Indiana. I spoke at the Labor of Love Infant Mortality Summit, and we allowed their rolling display of baby socks representing the children we had lost that year due to infant mortality to be displayed right outside of my office. Because of our personal experience of being on an adoption list and my support for pro-life causes, I always spoke at the adoption fair held at the Statehouse. Adoption fairs are a great way for organizations that promote adoption to come together and advertise what they can offer to families who may feel called to bring another child into their home through adoption.

As I think back over the many events I attended, I am reminded of the many causes that were brought to my attention and that I did my best to support. Being first lady truly expanded my focus. There were so many needs in Indiana that I had never realized existed.

I visited the Indiana Women's Prison and went to the Wee Ones Nursery Program, an extension of the prison's Family Preservation Program. The goal of the program is to break the cycle of incarceration by strengthening the mother-child bond earlier. These women are permitted to keep their babies that are born while they are incarcerated until their release rather than separating the mothers from their babies. I chatted with the women, held their babies, and encouraged these new young moms.

Art therapy also became a big part of my focus as first lady after I had gotten involved as a congressional spouse in the Tracy's Kids organization. I was asked to volunteer on the board of Riley Hospital for Children, and I concentrated my efforts on promoting the amazing art therapists there.

It was in July 2014, during my years as first lady, that my love affair with bees officially began. The Beekeepers of Indiana graciously donated and maintained our bees at the Governor's Residence. We harvested the honey each year and filled many little tiny honey-bear bottles with our honey. It made a great gift to give visitors to the Residence because honey never spoils. My staff and I put in many sticky hours filling those little bottles and I began to learn some of the many lessons the bees would teach me over the course of the years.

The culmination of my time as first lady revolved around Indiana's bicentennial, an important event in the life of our state. It was a special privilege for me to be first lady during the two hundredth year of our state's history. The Bicentennial Gala, which marked the culmination of our year-long celebration, was one of the last things I would do as first lady before our lives drastically changed once again.

I was asked by the Bicentennial Commission to be the ambassador and relished every moment of this time. Our goal on the commission was to have two hundred legacy projects, "projects highlighting the four pillars of the bicentennial effort: youth and education, historical celebration, community involvement and nature conservation,"*

---

* "Indiana Bicentennial Celebration 2016," IBC: Legacy Projects, https://www.in.gov/ibc/2351.htm.

around the state. We ended up having 1,650. My goal was to visit and highlight as many projects and counties as possible. I had so much fun with this! The projects were as varied as Hoosiers! They ranged from sampling bicentennial coffee, to visiting the Limestone Heritage Trail, to visiting the historic Leora Brown school. I also rode my bike along the Griffin Bike Park, dedicated to Sergeant Dale R. Griffin and established by his family, and toured the state to see a myriad of quilts in shops, quilt patterns made of wood displayed on barns, and even a quilt flower garden in northern Indiana. I was also able to encourage Hoosiers to participate in the Bicentennial Torch Relay, a twenty-three-hundred-mile journey across the state. Our state flag has a torch at the center of it so an Olympic-style torch relay seemed just the thing!

It was important to me to recognize this historic opportunity to help celebrate our state. I invited the members of the Indiana State Assembly Club to the Governor's Residence for an 1816 Bicentennial High Tea. These are spouses of our state legislators. We all dressed in period costume, complete with gloves and little hats. The ladies really got into it. I then went on to dress in that costume and travel to speak about Indiana to fourth-grade classrooms all over the state.

At the state fair that year, we even had a large display featuring decorated life-size "bison" from all over the state that had been creatively decorated for our "Bison-tennial art project exhibit."

I wanted to incorporate the bicentennial theme into the other projects/initiatives I had taken on as first lady. For our third First Lady's Luncheon, we wanted to really celebrate Indiana with the theme "Celebrating Indiana's Bicentennial." We presented our large check to the Bicentennial Commission with the intention of fully funding the interactive children's display at the Statehouse, "Treasures of the Statehouse." Our entertainer was Indiana's own Jon McLaughlin, singing his pop hit "Beating My Heart." The custom hand-blown glass bowl centerpieces in Indiana's colors of blue and gold were created by Kokomo Opalescent Glass.

We were just getting started planning our fourth luncheon when Mike was added to the national ticket as the vice presidential candidate, and we knew, win or lose, I wouldn't be first lady the next spring. So our fourth luncheon never came to fruition. But the women on the luncheon committee and the foundation were absolutely amazing. They made my job a joy and a privilege. I will forever be grateful for the countless hours they donated to such a worthy cause.

Indiana's two hundredth birthday was December 11, so on the evening of Saturday, December 10, much of Indiana celebrated the event at the Bicentennial Gala. The next morning there was a ceremony promoting our youth titled "Igniting the Future." This was truly a fitting way to end my time as first lady of Indiana, celebrating the many amazing Hoosiers and our fabulous state.

I will cherish my memories as Indiana's first lady. My goal was to be a good steward of the opportunity, to carry my load equal to 80 percent of my body weight as the bees do; I wanted to serve, I wanted to give something to my state . . . but in the end, I was the one who benefited from the rich, exhilarating experience. That's what happens so often when we take up the cause that God is calling us to . . . when it's our turn.

After that, things changed, and they changed quickly.

CHAPTER TEN

Running for VP

Honey bees fly as fast as 15 miles per hour.

In June 2016, Mike received a phone call from an acquaintance of ours who also was a friend of Donald Trump.

I had a friend from grade school, Karen Klee, who was in town visiting me at the time. I remember Mike coming home and telling me about the phone call. My friend and I were outside near the driveway at the Governor's Residence. We saw him pull up. He said he needed to talk to me, and I remember at the time feeling a little annoyed because I rarely get to see this friend, and I didn't want to take any time away from her visit. But he was clearly stunned by the call, so I asked him what was going on.

This man asked Mike if he would be willing to be considered as a running mate for Donald Trump.

This was kind of surprising because Mike hadn't even endorsed

Trump in the Indiana Republican primary. But we talked about it that evening and he got back to the mutual friend, saying he would be willing to be considered, even though it would mean he could not run for reelection as Indiana's governor if he were selected.

Mike said that for us to be able to make the decision to be on the national ticket if Donald Trump wanted to choose him, we would want to first meet the Trumps and get to know them as a family. We assumed that stipulation would rule us out because it was already June. And time was running out. But the Trumps did invite us to the Trump resort in Bedminster, New Jersey, to get to know the family. Charlotte came with us. We spent a few days, Mike played a round of golf with Donald Trump and two others, and we had dinner with them on the balcony restaurant of their club. Driving our little golf cart back to our room, we were certain Mike was not going to be the choice. Dinner had been very nice, but at the end, Trump told Mike he would be okay, that he would find a place for him in the administration. I thought that was a pretty clear indication that he was going in a different direction. After we left, we were at peace with whatever came next. We knew that our family would be together, that we would trust God, and we wouldn't "flap" to try to get to any position. But we couldn't have been more wrong about Trump's impression of Mike.

Everything happened very quickly. As Trump moved closer to making his final decision, he was interested in his kids meeting us as well. His plane had landed in Indianapolis, where he did a campaign event. Unfortunately, his plane had a flat tire, and it required him to spend the night in Indy, so he flew his kids to Indianapolis the next morning instead of us flying to New York to meet them.

We planned to have them over for breakfast at the Governor's Residence in Indiana. Remember, there is no chef or overnight staff at the Residence, so I went to work. I called my deputy chief of staff and Residence manager at 10 p.m. and asked her to reach out to the owner of the Illinois Street Emporium, a small local restaurant near the Residence that was one of our favorite places, to see if they could deliver six individual egg dishes and fruit salad the next morning to serve the Trumps. Mike and I went outside around 11 p.m. and picked flowers from the garden by the light of his cell phone, set the table, and prepared the coffee.

As it turned out, we had a lovely breakfast, and I think it meant something to the Trump family that the governor and first lady were serving breakfast and pouring coffee!

That night, Trump called Mike, and he and I went into a room together to take the call. Trump said, "Mike, it's gonna be great!" He continued talking about how Mike could go west and he would go east. Mike would go south and he would go north, etc. Mike said, "Well, Donald, if there's a question there, the answer is yes!"

Donald Trump had chosen Mike as his running mate, and we were suddenly thrown into a national campaign that had already been going on for years.

Once again, God was teaching me to let go of worthless idols. Yes, staying in Indiana and running for reelection as governor would have been the comfortable thing to do . . . I had this first lady thing down . . . but I opened my hands and let go (again) of the comfortable and made room for the challenging.

Our kids all agreed that someone needed to accompany Mom and Dad on the campaign trail, and Charlotte was the logical choice.

Audrey couldn't quit school, and Michael certainly couldn't leave the military. Charlotte was living in Indiana that summer and working at a local traveling summer camp. She left the job early and came with us on the trail to make sure we ate healthy and worked out at hotel gyms as she traveled everywhere with us. We had our own plane with TRUMP PENCE emblazoned across the fuselage. The flight attendants really got to know our whole team. We crisscrossed the United States, holding rallies and fundraisers everywhere we went. We traveled extensively, often to several states in just one day, holding multiple events and meeting people all over the country. Charlotte was on the trail with her dad even more days than I was.

A presidential campaign usually lasts about two years. With Mike being the vice presidential pick, we would be campaigning from July to November, about five months. The campaign trail was its own learning experience, too. Each day was typically a new city and schedule, so there were a lot of logistical things we had to get down. We figured out what we needed to pack each day, but we also had to go with the flow. We had a lot of ground to cover. Interestingly, the campaign never sent Charlotte or me out solo. While I would remind them, it never happened. Be that as it was, we had a lot of fun traveling all of us together.

On Halloween, the flight crew had decorated the cabin with Halloween flair. We all wore silly masks and had a great time together. It was a strange night, though, because during Mike's speech, the lights went out in the hangar where he was speaking to a crowd of supporters. Our staffers ended up shining a light on him and giving him a bullhorn to use as a microphone.

The campaign trail was an incredible experience. Even though we had been campaigning for years, it was different and it was amazing to see all of the people come out to support Donald Trump for president—and unlike anything we'd seen before in our political lives. People were so enthusiastic and excited. They lined the road wherever we went with signs and American flags. From small towns to big cities, this was clearly a movement that was sweeping the country, and we got to see it firsthand.

But my favorite part of all of it was just listening to people and hearing their concerns. We were told by countless individuals that it was their first time voting, or they knew someone who had never voted before but was going to come out to support Donald Trump. It was a very humbling experience. It reminded me of what I loved about politics when we first started so many years ago . . . people caring about their community and their nation. I was a listening ear to their concerns and their values, and I was happy to fill this role again. It seemed like so many people felt for the first time that someone was going to finally stand up for them, and they were connecting to Donald Trump in a very unique way. Everywhere we went the crowds were huge; people were inspired and hopeful!

I remember vividly one night when we were campaigning in Williamsburg, Virginia. It was pouring rain, but we went ahead with the event anyway. The outside venue in front of the historical Governor's Palace was packed with rain-soaked supporters. Due to security measures, they were not allowed to have umbrellas. But they didn't seem to care. They stood outside waiting for Mike to arrive. He gave a rip-roaring, enthusiastic speech, then we all headed back to the plane for dry towels and hot chocolate. We were all completely drenched and shivering. But to see all of those people so excited to be there was another very humbling and encouraging experience. Mike's speech cards—note cards he wrote his stump speech on—were also completely wet, so we spread them out all over the plane to dry on our way back home. One tradition we started early in the campaign was having everyone on the plane clap as soon as we touched down back in Indiana.

The hardest part of the campaign trail was probably the unknown. Here, we had made ourselves available to God to run for vice president, and meeting so many people all over the country was a wonderful experience. But still . . . the unknown was always in the back of my mind. *What are we going to do if we lose?* Sometimes, when we answer God's call, we really don't have any idea where it's going to take us. I guess that's where trust really comes in.

While campaigning was an enjoyable time, there were some moments that were more tense than others. One experience I don't think any of us will ever forget is the time our plane went off the runway while landing at LaGuardia Airport in New York. The weather was rainy that evening, but I don't think any of us thought anything about it. When we landed, we touched down too far down the runway. In order for us not to go through the fence at the end of the runway and onto the interstate, the pilot steered the plane off the runway onto the concrete berm on the side, which is created to break apart in order to help stop a plane. We didn't know that at the time. We only knew we had swerved and mud had splattered all over all of the windows. So we really didn't know exactly what had happened at first. Mike got up and went all the way through the plane making sure all of our staff and reporters traveling with us were all right. No one was hurt, just a bit shaken. Then he headed up to thank the pilots. According to our son, Michael, who is a pilot, too, they probably saved our lives with their quick action.

We traveled so much, we actually had a Styrofoam-backed map of the United States taped to the front of the cabin for everyone to see. It was a tradition I continued in my second lady office. We had a huge world map in the foyer of my office, riddled with little flags marking every place we had visited, with a different color of flag for my different initiatives. Every time we visited a city, we added a push pin to the map. It was unbelievable how many places we visited on the campaign trail. We held three rallies the night before the election, finishing in Michigan at a 1 a.m. rally early on the morning of Election Day. But eventually it all came to an end, and election night 2016 was upon us.

On election night, we were in New York City. Audrey was in Tanzania for an internship at the U.S. embassy for the semester. Michael, Sarah, and Charlotte were with us. People were watching the many television screens at the campaign office, tracking the progress throughout the night. Once the results were really starting to come in quickly, and we knew the outcome would be decided any moment, we huddled together in a tight circle and called Audrey. We needed to all be connected at this momentous occasion in our lives, as a family, one way or another. Mike and I had weathered nine elections together, seven of them with the kids. But this one would significantly affect all of us individually.

As it began to be clear that we really might win, we all headed to the Trumps' home, where the president-elect was finalizing his remarks. There had been stacks of boxes of pizza at the campaign headquarters, but none of us had felt like eating at the time. Now it was getting late, and we were all starving. Some of our amazing advance staffers offered to go get food, and we quickly agreed. The kids went down to the vehicles and ate while Mike and I stayed upstairs.

That night ended up being a very late one. Many of our family and friends and supporters had stayed right where they were all night in the ballroom where Trump would give his acceptance speech. Their support was amazing! Once Hillary Clinton conceded, we all headed out onto the stage to mark this momentous occasion! All of the long hours, travel, and campaigning had paid off.

Mike was going to be the forty-eighth vice president of the United States. And I was going to be the second lady. I realized once again that here was an opportunity, just like being a congressional spouse or first lady, to take up my baton, to wear the mantle God was placing on my shoulders. He had certainly shown me He would be next to me the entire way. I had so many examples to look back on as I stepped into these shoes. It reminded me to trust Him. Once again, I was reminded of the verse I love in Deuteronomy where God is reprimanding the Israelites for not trusting Him, even though He had carried them through the wilderness. Deuteronomy 1:29–32 says, "Then I said to you, 'Do not be terrified; do not be afraid of them. The LORD your God, who is going before you, will fight for you, as he did for you in Egypt, before your very eyes, and in the desert. There you saw how the LORD your God carried you, as a father carries his son, all the way you went until you reached this place.' In spite of this, you did not trust in the LORD your God." I didn't want to be like the Israelites. I didn't want to grumble or let fear or anxiety rule my thoughts. So I focused, as I have many times in my life, on the section "the Lord your God carried you, as a father carries his son, all the way you went until you reached this place . . ." God had carried me all this way, and now He was taking us back to D.C., carrying us as a father carries his son, again. It was going to be okay . . . that much I knew.

CHAPTER ELEVEN

Moving Back to D.C.

Honeybees beat their wings two hundred times each second, which makes their trademark "buzz" sound.

We were moving back to Washington, D.C., and creating quite a "buzz." I kept thinking, *Okay, Lord, I'm trusting you.* As Proverbs 3:5–6 says, "Lean not on your own understanding; in all your ways acknowledge Him, and He will make your paths straight."

I think we were all still fairly numb after the election results came in. The last time I lived in D.C., I was an art teacher heading home to Indiana, and now I was returning to become the second lady of the United States. One part of me felt very comfortable, since I had lived in this city for twelve years, but another part of me realized things were never going to be the same. As tradition goes, the sitting vice president sends Air Force Two to bring the vice president–elect, along with his or her family, to Washington, D.C. Mike, Charlotte, and I boarded one of the Air Force Two planes in Indiana, with our pets in tow and not many belongings, to make the trip to D.C. The few personal items we still owned were packed up to make the trek from Indiana to Washington, D.C. There was a little bit of time where we would be in limbo with regard to our living situation. From January 9 to January 20, our items stayed in storage in a moving truck because that was the time between the swearing-in of the new governor of Indiana and the inauguration of Mike as vice president. One treasured item that has always moved with us since the year 2000 is a framed scripture verse of Jeremiah 29:11, which reads, "'For I know the plans I have for you,' says the Lord. 'Plans to prosper you and not to harm you. Plans to give you a hope and a future.'" If I ever had to trust in that verse, now was the time.

For me, thankfully, Washington was a familiar place. I had friends; I knew where the bank was; I knew my way around; I was at home on Capitol Hill; I had my favorite "hangouts." So I wasn't intimidated about returning to our nation's capital. It had been our home away from home for twelve years. God had called us there before, and He was calling us back, and I had to trust Him that He knows what is best for me and my family.

When we arrived in Washington, D.C., we stayed in a rental home the transition team rented for us in Maryland and got busy hiring staff, setting up systems, and establishing our offices once again. We'd been through this before in a way, but on a different scale. We'd also been through the process of moving into a rental home during a transitional period. This rental home was filled with several boxes lining the halls, which had gowns and clothes for us to wear for two weeks before we were reconnected with the rest of our belongings. It was a beautiful home, and it featured an entire wall of windows in the family room. The first day we walked in, however, we noticed the Secret Service had put brown paper over every single window to increase the security of the house. It was a little bit of a rude awakening. Our life was different now.

During the transition period, our staff was busy planning the inauguration. The Indiana Society of Washington, D.C., hosts an Inaugural Ball, complete with a sit-down dinner and dancing the night before the inauguration, of which I had been the honorary chair for the last three inaugurations. I had served on this board in the past, and here I was, in a new role as the honored guest with Mike. It was a bit surreal. We hired the same woman who had made my wedding gown and my gown for the gubernatorial inauguration to make my and Charlotte's and Audrey's and Sarah's gowns for the inaugural events. There were a lot of events that week, and honestly it was a little difficult keeping them all straight. I remember hearing of one dinner just a few days before it was going to occur, and Charlotte and I headed out to a local mall to find a gown for each of us to wear at the last minute!

The inauguration was extremely complex. There were dinners, luncheons, everything surrounding the swearing-in, including the lunch in Statuary Hall at the Capitol afterward, the church service at St. John's, and more. There were inaugural gifts, invitations, transportation, hotel accommodations, security badges, and other things to keep track of.

Jill and Joe Biden had given us a tour of the Vice President's Residence (VPR) in November. It was top to bottom, except for one closet that Jill asked Joe not to show us where she had a lot of things stored. We had a lovely lunch cooked by the Naval Enlisted Aides. The Bidens graciously allowed me to take pictures so that I could plan what furniture we would need. Four years later, due to Covid, we did not tour Kamala Harris and Doug Emhoff. But Doug and I had a great conversation before they took office where I tried to answer as many questions as I could.

For my part, I was planning a brunch at the Vice President's Residence for the morning after the inauguration. That was a little tricky, trying to make sure we included close friends and family in a home where I hadn't even moved in yet. Trying to manage security clearance for all of the people who would attend the brunch was a difficult task for the transition staff, and after the brunch, we had arranged for a tour of the U.S. Naval Observatory. The Vice President's Residence is a special place to live, with the Naval Observatory right across the street from the Residence! That night, climbing the stairs in the observatory to look up at the universe reminded me of how small we are, and how vast God's creation is. He is bigger than my little fears and insecurities, and I knew He would guide me through this new chapter just as he had in the past.

I now needed to turn my attention to my own office and my own team. I wanted my office to be very welcoming to all the visitors I knew we were going to have over the years. But I also knew I needed a top-notch team. Our budget was limited, and we had a small staff.

I had hired people before as first lady of Indiana, and what I learned from that experience was that you really are only as good as your people, and I had had some amazing people as first lady. Now the stakes were higher. There would be eight people, and not only did they have to be excellent in their own positions, but they also needed to work well as a team. For the entire four years, I always reminded them to stay in their own lane. I hired people who were excellent at their skill set, and I knew it was important for their own confidence that no one else would be allowed to infringe on their space. That is a fine balance to maintain when you hire people who are good at so many things, but it's something I insisted upon even up to the very last day.

The first person I hired on my team was my communications director, Kara Brooks, who had worked in the press office in the governor's office when Mike was governor. Hiring someone who already knew me and had worked for us in Indiana and was a Hoosier really gave me a sense of peace. I knew she could handle whatever the press threw at her. She also could write my speeches in my voice, which is so important. When she was interviewing for the job, she studied my first lady speeches and wrote some sample speeches trying to mimic the way I speak. So on day one, I knew I had someone qualified for that very important position. My second hire was my policy director, Sara Egeland. She impressed me because she had been the sole full-time staffer for another first lady, so she understood where we were coming from, and she was very capable. As time went on, she proved she could master any issue and keep me fully up to speed.

For a while, it was just the three of us. I remember late one night, we moved furniture around in the Eisenhower Executive Office Building, trying to make sure that we would be all set up and our office would be ready to go on day one. We were just about the only ones in the building. We would go from room to room to see if there might be a stray chair that matched what we had or a lamp that might fit on a lone table. It was a fun adventure that the three of us would remember fondly from time to time. Both of them were with me to the very last day.

While we were setting up the office, we had a lot of fun and learned quickly that there is a procedure for everything. Since it's a historical building, the office had been restored back to its original paint, which is very elaborate. We were trying to match window treatments and hang some pictures, but we weren't allowed to hammer nails in the wall because of preservation efforts for the building, so everything was hung from the ceiling with fishing line. I do believe the Office of the Second Lady is the nicest office in Washington because it has a beautiful balcony looking out onto the White House lawn and the Washington Monument. We had many events and staff lunches out there.

Our goal was to be ready to go on day one, and we really were. The offices were set up . . . now we just needed to staff them! As a classroom teacher and an art teacher, I sometimes had a teacher's assistant, but I was mostly on my own. I could see how God had prepared me while I was first lady and had three staff members, for this moment of leading eight new staff members. He had slowly transitioned me to this new position. While it might have been intimidating to go from art teacher to second lady, it was not intimidating to make the jump from first lady of Indiana to second lady of the United States. God had gently helped me grow into this role. When He calls us, he prepares us and He walks the new path with us.

My first chief of staff, Kristan Nevins, had agreed to be my chief of staff for just the first year to get me set up. She'd been Barbara Bush's chief of staff after Mrs. Bush left the White House, and Barbara Bush sent me a very nice note congratulating me on hiring her! Mrs. Bush also mentioned in that same note that while she was second lady, she got up every day intending to do something good for someone, and the press never paid any attention to her. But as soon as her husband, George H. W. Bush, became the nominee for president, her tongue started getting her in trouble, and it had gotten her in trouble ever since. I was grateful for her candor and sense of humor. I'm so glad I had the privilege of knowing her.

God had even prepared me for that relationship many years before. When Mike was first running for Congress, I had the privilege of being invited to the Vice President's Residence and then again once he was elected. My first visit was when Barbara Bush was the second lady. She was very gracious and she took many pictures with all of us. I remember when she addressed our group of candidate spouses from the landing in the foyer. As she was speaking, Millie, their Cocker Spaniel, came moseying down the stairs behind her. We all let out an audible sigh. She looked behind her, realizing Millie must have come down the steps. She said in her humorous way, "Ladies, she's just a dog." She went on to share that she had moved with George twenty-five times, and said it had made for a very rich life. She encouraged us to do the same. I never forgot her words of wisdom, and I took her words to heart. I cherished the photos with her, and I kept one of those pictures on the grand piano at the Vice President's Residence the whole four years we lived there. I also kept a photo of Marilyn Quayle skipping with our girls along a small Indiana tarmac when she campaigned for us after she had been second lady. Lynn Cheney also invited the congressional spouses to visit when she was second lady. She graciously toured us all out by the pool that the Quayles had installed using private money.

When Mrs. Bush passed away during Mike's time as vice president, I brought Kristan a bouquet of lilacs from the Residence that Mrs. Bush had planted around the VPR flagpole.

Being second lady would not only entail duties promoting my initiatives, but there would be several official responsibilities as well. I frequently would host the spouse of a visiting dignitary. I especially remember Akie Abe, the first lady of Japan. She and the late Prime Minister Shinzo Abe loved their dogs. I have a sweet photo of her and me laughing hysterically as she plays fetch with our dog, Harley.

There were many special events held at the White House. These ranged from official lunches to Gold Star ceremonies, as well as dinners and entertainment with our nation's governors. The annual White House Congressional Christmas Ball was a must-attend event, as well as the French and Australian state dinners. Participating in each of these events and many others was always a privilege.

These events were another way for me to try to be the best steward and servant I could be in this new and unconventional role. I met people from all over the world and enjoyed getting to know so many interesting people. God was stretching me, and I enjoyed it.

We also would be hosting lots of events at the Vice President's Residence. I hired two employees who would work full-time at the Residence. My Residence manager was Cynthia Andrade, who had been in the catering business for many years. She served me very well the entire four years with the many events we held at the VPR while we lived there. After we left office, I invited her to my own Christmas party back in Indiana and asked her how she thought I had done. She had taught me well how to entertain on a large scale. Kristan, my chief of staff, helped me round out the positions, and we were up and running. My second chief of staff, Jana Toner, truly kept us focused on military families and using every opportunity we had. She was very creative at juggling our small budget and staff. Her extensive experience in the George W. Bush administration and elsewhere in government really served me well. All of the people who worked for me as first lady and second lady had such incredible hearts for service. They loved their jobs, and it showed. They made me look good; they served our country with honor and I am so grateful to have had them.

There's a great visual in Exodus 17:10–12. "So Joshua fought the Amalekites as Moses had ordered, and Moses, Aaron and Hur went to the top of the hill. As long as Moses held up his hands, the Israelites were winning, but whenever he lowered his hands, the Amalekites were winning. When Moses' hands grew tired, they took a stone and put it under him and he sat on it. Aaron and Hur held his hands up—one on one side, one on the other—so that his hands remained steady till sunset."

These dedicated staff held up my hands.

CHAPTER TWELVE

Secret Service

*Guard bees actually guard the entrance to the hive
so they can sense intruders (like bees from different
hives), which they frequently do by smell.*

The United States Secret Service started protecting us the day Mike
was officially added to the Republican ticket at the Republican National Convention in Cleveland in July 2016, but they took over
full force in November after the election was over. He was now not
just a candidate, but the vice president–elect. Max Milien was the
one constant Secret Service agent who was with us from our first
day up until our very last.

Having Secret Service protection is a humbling experience. These
are dedicated men and women who have lives and families of their
own, but who choose for many hours during the day or night to protect my family and me, to be there if I am in danger. Working with
the Secret Service is an intricate dance. For me, the loss of privacy

was the hardest part of being second lady. There was always some-one standing a few feet away from me no matter what I was doing (including standing outside my art classroom when I was teaching). I am a very private person, so this was difficult for me. Even though we'd had a security detail during our time as governor and first lady, this was on a much larger level.

I learned quickly that things were going to be different now. I tried to rent a vacation condo our first spring in office and was told that the Secret Service would need to install bulletproof glass, sweep all condos in the building, set up a roadblock, and have dogs sniff each car entering the complex. Needless to say, that was a wake-up call and I canceled the condo. I remember being very dis-couraged at the time. I had no idea how we could get away for a change of scenery while Mike was vice president. The president has Camp David and his own home. During our time in the vice pres-ident's office, we didn't have a home of our own. We were grateful that the Indiana governor, Eric Holcomb, and Janet Holcomb al-lowed us to occasionally stay at Aynes House in Indiana. I knew that, from time to time, it would do Mike good to at least be in a different environment, even though as vice president, you never are really on vacation. So this was another thing I needed to think through. I honestly had no idea how I was going to figure this out. So I asked my prayer support team in Indiana to pray for me.

When I was first lady of Indiana, I had assembled a group of five women who met with me weekly at the Governor's Residence to pray for each other. We would gather in a small sitting room off of the first floor kitchen. The housekeeper, Candee, would prepare some breakfast treats and coffee and tea, and we would all share prayer requests and then actually take the time right then to pray for those requests. One thing I learned early on was that when I was going to be in a position of leadership, I needed all the prayer cover I could get! This group continued throughout the vice presidential years via email, and we still share weekly prayer requests and gather in person when we can. It has been a great source of comfort for all of us. I also have two dear friends in Washington who have been my prayer partners since 2003. We get together when we can, but we pray over the phone almost every week. We have kept prayer journals over the years, and it is such a blessing to go back and see how God has answered prayers for our families since our children were very little. Having a safe place where I can be vulnerable and completely trust my friends to be discreet has been a tremendous blessing.

When I learned from the Secret Service that for all practical purposes, I could not rent a vacation home, I added this dilemma in my prayer request email to the Indiana group. We had been trying to spend our vacation on Sanibel Island in Florida and had loved going there as a family for many years in the past. We started going to Sanibel as a family after Mike's father passed away, and it became a place near and dear to us and then to our kids once they came along. We've always loved going to that little island and were deeply saddened to see the devastation that took place after Hurricane Ian hit Florida just a few years later. Mike and I went down to Sanibel over Thanksgiving of 2022 to encourage the people there. As always, I was inspired by the resilience of the people who were putting their lives back together, and I know Sanibel will continue to be a very special place for us, and while we were serving as vice president and second lady, we found a lot of solace there.

When I shared this predicament with my prayer group, I learned that the in-laws of one of my friends' daughters owned a home on Sanibel Island, and they were frequently out of town. Reese and Linda Kauffman ran an international ministry for children, and had a home provided by the ministry in another state. My friend Julie

Brown reached out to them, and they were more than gracious to allow us to stay in their Sanibel home several times while Mike was vice president. The Secret Service loved the isolated location of the house, and the Coast Guard patrolled twenty-four hours out in the water in front of the property. This home and these wonderful people were a Godsend! God provided, just like He always does. It still was very strange having a group of agents standing under a tent for shade nearby when I was sitting on the beach, and even though I knew we needed them there, I never really got used to them.

One weekend, we went to visit my best friend and her husband, Karen and Larry Klee, in Montana. It was quite an ordeal to have agents staying in cabins nearby that belonged to friends of our friends who weren't occupying their cabins that weekend. Fly fishing along the banks of the river, seeing agents in scuba gear ready to rescue the VP should he fall in the fast-moving river was a little disconcerting. All types of security measures were in place, from the top of the bluffs nearby, to the little church we attended, to driving through the creek instead of going over the bridge due to the weight of the armored vehicles. Just a weekend out in the wilderness . . .

Back in D.C., agents also patrolled in front of the porch at the Vice President's Residence. I remember Mike asking them once, when we were sitting on the beautiful wraparound porch catching up, to please make a wider loop so we could have a little privacy. There is a small road that circles the entire property. And there were twelve deer living inside the seventy-two fenced acres when we lived there. (Mike called them the "dirty dozen.") To feel like we had a little freedom, some evenings, Mike and I would take the VPR golf cart out for a spin around the property with Harley. Secret Service followed us in their golf cart. They followed me in stores; they sat near me in restaurants; they accompanied me on walks, five feet behind me; they came with me when I was helping my kids move; and they drove me everywhere. I missed driving myself with the windows down and the radio playing. Probably the most difficult aspect was that their duty rotations changed constantly, so just when I would get to know my team, they would shift, and I would be assigned a completely new group. And there were so many of them, especially where I was teaching, that I occasionally didn't recognize my own team since they rotated so frequently. I sometimes wondered if the bad guys had taken over my Secret Service detail, and if I was getting into the car with someone I shouldn't. They assured me that wasn't going to happen, but it was a little disconcerting, to say the least. I'd often poke my head into the front of the vehicle and ask what the agent's name was, just to get a little more familiar with the people who were spending my days with me.

Even though having them full-time was difficult, it was essential. Once, one of them explained to a friend of mine that it was imperative to keep the four principals (the president, vice president, first lady, and second lady) safe and secure at all times. If something would happen, it would affect not only the United States, but the world. And honestly, it is a difficult existence for them as well. I got to know several of them and learned about their families, who make so many sacrifices for them to serve in this job. It isn't easy for them, either. On an impulse, we might decide we want to go on a bike ride, so they suddenly needed to map out a route. Or I would need to drive hours to help move my kids, and they would need to go as well. This affected their home lives and schedules, too. Their families had to constantly adjust to our changing schedules as well. They also move frequently. As they move up the ranks of the Secret Service, they get reassigned, just like in the military.

At one of our last Christmas parties at the Vice President's Residence, all of the guests were Secret Service families. Having spent

My fascination with
bees began in February
2012. Over the years, the
bees have taught me more
and more about myself
and God's creation.

On Monday nights, when our son was just a baby,
I would attend a watercolor class to hone my skills. This
rocking chair painting was done during those classes.

Facing page: This painting went on to be entered in an art
show in Brown County, Indiana, where it received an honorable
mention. I am grateful that many of my watercolors
have been exhibited at the Indiana State Fair.

Karen Dancic

The Capitol dome print was painted in 2010 while Mike was
still in Congress. It has been used as a gift in print form and as
notecards, and reminds me of our time serving in Washington,
D.C., and of the many experiences we shared as a family.

Mike filmed a commercial on this property in Bartholomew County, Indiana, and loved the front porch so much that he asked me to paint it to hang in his congressional office. We made every effort to hold fast to our Indiana roots, and he wanted this painting in his office to remind him of home.

Mike hadn't even run for governor yet when I painted
the Governor's Residence for a group that was holding a fundraiser there.
By then I had developed quite a business creating paintings of peoples'
homes, and the organizer of the event had seen my work.
Little did I know that I'd live in the Residence one day!

Our family created many special
memories at Aynes House, the
Indiana governor's retreat.

The peony is Indiana's state flower.
This painting was featured at the inaugural Indiana
First Lady's Luncheon in 2013, which raised
funds for the Indiana First Lady's Charitable
Foundation. The foundation, in turn, awarded
grants to charities in all ninety-two counties.

*The Indiana Ball Jar With
Wildflowers* was created
for the 2015 Indiana First
Lady's Luncheon.

Marlon Bundo was
quite the diva. He loved posing
for pictures that I would later use to
paint watercolors for his first book,
A Day in the Life of the Vice President.
The picture for the watercolor
to the left was taken by Amelia
Cassar, my daughter Charlotte's
good friend and photographer.

Some of the watercolors from that book
include Marlon peeking out at the Capitol dome
from the limo, the vice president holding Marlon
in his West Wing office, and Marlon at the
entrance to the West Wing. Marlon's books were
a joy for Charlotte and me to do together.

Marlon's second book focused on Marlon spending
A Day in the Nation's Capital. These watercolors show him visiting
the Vietnam Memorial, the South Lawn of the White House, the
Lincoln Memorial, and the Iwo Jima Memorial—all special places
to our family after having lived in Washington so many years.

My children attended picnics on the White House South Lawn when they were young. The Lincoln Memorial was one of our favorite memorials to visit over and over again. The vice president and I spent one Veterans Day cleaning the Vietnam Memorial in honor of our lost soldiers.

I originally made this painting of the Naval Observatory because
I have painted almost every one of our homes, so it seemed fitting to paint
the Vice President's Residence. We had prints made that we gave to every
second family. It was an honor to live there and create cherished memories.

I loved painting the Second Family Christmas
card each year that Mike was vice president. We
replicated these images into an ornament that
we gave to all our guests for the holiday.

The Cardinal in Snow was originally created as a Christmas print when Mike was governor. I later gave it as a print to all the athletes participating in the Special Olympics World Winter Games in Austria that I attended as second lady, which was the highlight of my time in that position.

I painted these hummingbird watercolors to be
used as gifts, as my Secret Service codename was
"Hummingbird." When Mike and I—"Hoosier"
and "Hummingbird"—headed back to Indiana,
my daughter, Charlotte, gave me a poem
she had written while at graduate school.

her bees will stay
feed the flowers, keep them going,
appreciate the ones planted just for them,
they have a home here, but the wind decides where they flit,
they promise her they will keep it up,
hunting for the perfect slice
moving toiling sweating
coming home from a long day,
put their feet up and hold hands after dinner by the fire,
picking a television show is always a task
then it's too late and off to bed again,
turn off the lights and know
that tomorrow's work still means something,
even unseen,
they did their best, do their best, now rest;
i love you, goodnight,
ignore those outside,
eyeing the hive

—Charlotte Pence Bond

four years with these dedicated men and women by my side at all hours, I wanted to take the opportunity to tell them how much my family appreciated them and their service to us over the four years while Mike was vice president. As I've articulated, it isn't easy to get used to such a lack of privacy that full-time security creates, but the fact that those men and women would come to work each day to protect my family, my husband, and me was truly more humbling than I can describe. I wanted to address them all as a group. I wanted their families to hear what great people they are. What follows is an abbreviated version of my remarks that night.

Welcome to the safest place you could be in Washington tonight!

This is a special night for us, to be able to honor those from the United States Secret Service who protect us every day, all day. . . .

We know that we aren't always the most appreciative when you all are driving us around. We are distracted, making phone calls, catching up on work in the car . . . so we don't always—okay, we rarely—say thank you. So tonight we are saying, "thank you."

Thank you to the agents. Thank you to the spouses. Thank you to the families. We know it is tough duty being part of the Secret Service. We know if we are gone at Christmas, you are gone from your families at Christmas. And that is no fun. So thank you.

Tonight I want the spouses and children to hear a few stories. . . .

My first rescue by an agent was while I was walking through Lucas Oil Stadium at an Indianapolis Colts game in Indiana. My agent was Pete. He was walking right behind me. And suddenly, I slipped on some pudding and Pete caught me! I remember saying, "Nice catch, Pete!" You all are trained to have razor-sharp instincts. . . . Like the guys who are the drivers. I've had a few occasions where my driver has avoided a serious accident with their quick instincts. My drivers are great. It's always a treat to get in the car and say, "Pete! Lou! Frank! Great to see you!" However, I don't have that affinity for the VP's drivers. Here is why . . . It's fun riding in a VP motorcade once. Then you learn to just hold on as these guys swerve left and right keeping us safe.

I can't really say our kids enjoyed having a security detail. College kids don't want an adult following them around. Right, Max? They don't want an agent on their dates . . . at their parties . . . outside their classroom. They don't want the Secret Service going with them on their study abroad trips. Right, Max? Audrey and Max worked through some tricky arrangements and complicated situations and dangerous environments.

When our daughter decided to get married on November 1st, 2020, two days before the 2020 presidential election, because her wedding had been postponed due to Covid three times, she had one agent she especially wanted to be there making sure it would be safe. Right, Max?

And one day near the end of October, when I was in Indianapolis campaigning, I found out Audrey had finally gotten an appointment at a wedding dress salon back in Washington. They had given us a two-week notice that they wanted to go ahead and get married November 1, and she didn't have a dress. It was ten days before the wedding. No one on my detail knew about the upcoming wedding. We were trying to keep it very secret. I asked Andy, my lead, if he could try to *get me to the airport (with no lights or sirens . . .) but could we try to catch the earlier flight? He didn't know, but I wanted to be with her when she got her wedding dress. We made it to the flight, only to sit on the tarmac for an hour due to a lightning storm. When we finally landed at Dulles Airport, I told the new agent, "Guys, don't tell anyone . . . but I'm trying to get to a bridal salon before they close because Audrey is getting her wedding dress. No lights or sirens, but can you try to get me there?" And that night, Audrey and I walked out with her dress. You all play a more important role than you will ever realize.*

Max is also the agent who was on duty a few months ago when he had to tell us, "I'm sorry, but you can't go have dinner at Audrey's apartment tonight to see it for the first time because there may be riots tonight." This was the first night of protests in Washington. He said they had extra precautions in place here at the Residence that we wouldn't even notice, but they had heightened security. He knew I was disappointed we couldn't go to Audrey's that night. She had made a special dinner, cleaned her apartment, and walked through security protocols the day before with an agent. But that paled in comparison to the fact that men and women were putting themselves at risk right here at the Naval Observatory to make sure we were safe, to make sure the vice president was secure. There was a higher cause that we are dedicated to, and all of our great Secret Service agents are dedicated to it, too.

So Max has been a constant, but unfortunately I learned the hard way in 2017 that our detail agents rotate in and out pretty quickly. Just about the time we start to trust our lead, just about the time they get used to our routine, including standing outside my art room all day, they move on. And that has been hard. Sometimes we see them again when we're in Atlanta (Malcolm), or Philly (Chris), or Charlotte (Wade), or Indy (James). It's like seeing an old friend.

You all don't really know Mike and Karen Pence, "Hoosier and Hummingbird." Yet, you are willing to risk your lives to protect ours, to protect the United States of America.

So tonight, we want to say thank you.

Thank you to the agents, the drivers, the families.

Merry Christmas!

Max would also be the last agent we saw as we walked through the doors at the Capitol and down the red carpeted steps to attend the inauguration on January 20, 2021. I remember giving him a little wave as he continued his job of now protecting Kamala Harris, who was waiting to descend the steps and take her oath.

Having Secret Service protection was one of the most difficult parts of being second lady, but it was also very humbling. These people risk their lives every day, coming to work without knowing what might happen, to keep me and my family safe. But it's not really about us. That's the humbling part. With every new administration, the Secret Service protects the new principals and their families. It's an incredible part of our country's system, and it's an important part in preserving the stability of government, but the day-to-day was difficult. It made me appreciate everything that makes our system of government so successful.

CHAPTER THIRTEEN

Vice President's Residence

Bees are entirely self-sufficient. A bee colony can
eat about 120–200 pounds of honey each year.

With each incoming vice presidential family, the Vice President's Residence Foundation raises private money to furnish the home. The new vice presidents typically don't want the used furniture from the previous administration in the personal quarters. It would be like moving into a new home and the previous tenants had left all of their furniture. Therefore, at the end of an administration, a professional furniture appraiser comes to the house and evaluates each individual item. The outgoing vice president has the opportunity to purchase whatever items they want to take with them by writing a personal check to the Vice President's Residence Foundation. We had been told that there weren't many pieces of furniture remaining on the second and third floors where the family quarters are. Four years later when we moved out, we purchased the bedroom furniture and the family room furniture. These familiar pieces were a comfort to us as we first moved to a rental house and then later bought our permanent home in Indiana.

One of the unique things about the Vice President's Residence, or the VPR as it is known, is that there are no public tours for security reasons, so people are always curious about what it is like to live there. As I've mentioned, the house sits on the grounds of the U.S. Naval Observatory, and ever since Walter Mondale was vice president under Jimmy Carter, 1977–81, it has been used as a place for the vice president to live. It was originally meant to be used by the superintendent of the Naval Observatory, but the chief of naval operations decided he wanted it for himself in 1923. Congress consented to renovate the house in 1974 and make it a place where the vice president could live. The house is technically owned by the Navy, and the Navy is responsible for maintaining the house and property, so the daily management falls to the Naval Enlisted Aides, who are in charge of running it much like they would a Navy ship. They directly answer to the vice president, and we grew fond of many of our aides during our time at the VPR.

Once we had been elected, we were informed we could move into the Residence on January 20, the day Mike would be sworn in. That is the same day that we would be attending the inaugural balls. Kind of a lot . . . *being at your husband's swearing-in as vice president, moving, attending inaugural balls in the evening, and also hosting 150 guests at the Residence the next morning!* Our personal furniture by then, as I've explained, was very limited. Charlotte had flown out with me to meet with a decorator and purchase the furniture for the Residence. We chose items that were in stock and could be available by early January. We also needed to furnish bedrooms for our kids. The decorator and our moving company took copious notes, detailing where each picture would hang, where each item would be placed, and which closets and cabinets would contain what. We also needed painting to be done and carpeting to be installed after the Bidens moved out. It was a very busy time. On January 20, when we arrived home after the inaugural luncheon in Statuary Hall at the Capitol, every single thing was in its place. The Naval Enlisted Aides were ready to assist us in preparing for the evening, and it was truly a magical moment. Many of the same aides would return to salute us as we departed four years later. Our same moving company would come pack us up to move us to yet another rental once we left office.

We moved to the Residence with our cats, Pickle and Oreo, and our bunny, Marlon. Marlon had been Charlotte's bunny in college. She had gotten him on Craigslist to use in a film project for a class at DePaul University. She asked the owner how much the bunny cost, and got the response, "Make me an offer." This reminded her and her friends of Marlon Brando's line from *The Godfather*, "I'm gonna make him an offer he can't refuse." So she named him Marlon Bundo.

When Air Force Two brought us from Indiana to Washington, D.C., before the inauguration, the pets were all with us on the plane. As we got off the plane, one of our advance team leaders carried Marlon's cage, with Marlon inside, down the steps. For some reason, the fact that we had a bunny as a pet created quite a stir in the media. There were articles written about the vice president's bunny, Marlon. This prompted Charlotte to create an Instagram page for him and call it "marlonbundo." We gave him the nickname "Botus," "Bunny of the United States," as Dan, Audrey's boyfriend (and later husband), had suggested.

Marlon had become quite famous, having over thirty thousand followers on Instagram. Charlotte is our author. She decided she wanted to do a book featuring Marlon. We realized that when our own family suddenly found ourselves as the Second Family, there was a lot we didn't know about the vice presidency. So Charlotte researched and wrote a precious children's book in rhyme explaining what a day is like for the vice president, including all of his different duties. Her first book was *A Day in the Life of the Vice President*. She asked me to illustrate it. That was so much fun because Marlon, as it turned out, was quite the ham. We would set him in a pose, and Charlotte's friend Amelia, who is a professional photographer who was visiting, took a myriad of photos for me to use for my illustrations. We subsequently published *A Day in the Nation's Capital*, as well as *Marlon Bundo's Best Christmas Ever*. When we went on the book tour for the first book, we brought Marlon with us and he went on TV shows like *The View* and *Fox & Friends*. It was a lot of fun and so great to do it together.

On the morning of the first book's publication, Charlotte woke up to see a lot of activity on Marlon's social media account. Confused, she looked up some of the things people were posting, and she quickly discovered that the comedian John Oliver had published his own book parodying ours. It was a surprise, but we took it with a grain of salt and went on to do the book tour—and sell a lot of books. But Marlon didn't really like traveling, so he only did personal appearances for the first book, preferring to stay at the VPR for the following book tours.

The second book was all about Washington, D.C., and it had many historical lessons about different monuments around the city. For the illustrations, we used the Marlon Bundo prototype I had created in case we decided to include a stuffed bunny with the book sales. It had been created to look exactly like Marlon, with all of his cute little black markings, and we placed it in positions by the monuments, taking pictures for me to paint later on. It was very fun, and a little boy even grabbed the stuffed Marlon off the floor at the Lincoln Memorial and wanted to take it with him. We had the Secret Service drive us around and would jump out at a good location so we could get the right picture we needed for the book.

The last one we published was a Christmas book, where Marlon attends a holiday party at the Residence and learns all about the different members of staff who work there, from the military bands who would perform for our parties, to the Secret Service, to the pilots on Air Force Two. He crafts a special ornament that is composed of little pieces from around the house, including wax from the menorah and honey from the bees and glitter from the decorations. It was a lot of fun to make these together, and it was a way for Charlotte and me to stay connected. She was living and working in Los Angeles, where she would also write her book *Where You Go: Life Lessons from My Father*. She then moved to Massachusetts later on to pursue her master's degree in theology from Harvard, so it was a great project to work on long-distance.

Our pets have always been a main part of our life, from before we even had kids to our time in Congress to living at the Vice President's Residence. When I think about the VPR, our adventures with them stick out in my memory. Pickle, Oreo, and Marlon Bundo quickly endeared themselves to staff and visitors alike.

Oreo, in particular, attended each event welcoming guests, as well as making herself at home on top of our Residence manager's keyboard in the staff office. She is in several official photographs from events. I remember her walking across the back of the couch in the formal living room at a Women in Military event I hosted early on. She was right in the middle of the tweet! She seemed to position herself exactly in the right spot to end up in everyone's photo! Pickle was very old, and took on the role of "grandma cat." She was elderly and had diabetes, so it was more difficult for her to make it up and down the stairs.

To give you an idea of our lack of privacy, the day Pickle died, after calling Charlotte to tearfully inform her, Mike called down to the NEAs (Naval Enlisted Aides) to ask for a shovel. We explained that we would be digging a hole for Pickle in the garden. The maintenance guys offered to do it, but we said that we preferred to do it ourselves. Shortly after that, before Charlotte had even had a chance to tell her siblings of Pickle's passing, Mike's staff reached out and asked us if we wanted to do a tweet for Pickle. Word spreads quickly at the Residence, and it was a little disconcerting. Of course, people were just trying to be helpful, but we were struggling for any opportunity to keep a little normalcy in our lives. Unfortunately, shortly after Pickle passed, we noticed Oreo getting sick. A few days later, Oreo was much worse, and we put her in the hospital. Audrey came back home once we knew Oreo wasn't going to make it. Mike raced to meet Audrey and me at the vet, and the three of us were together as Audrey held Oreo in her final moments and we all cried.

I remember the Secret Service standing in the hallway at the vet, hearing us. There truly wasn't much privacy during these years. Walking to our car after this terrible moment, there were people outside taking pictures of us. We obviously were distraught, and we obviously were holding a box with our deceased pet inside. It seemed very insensitive, and Audrey asked them to respect our privacy.

We are pet people, and the big house at One Observatory Circle was very empty without our kitties.

For Mike's first Father's Day as vice president, the kids decided to get him a dog. We told Mike we were getting a new cat, but what he didn't know was we were also going to surprise him with a puppy. We all had traveled home to Indiana for a family wedding. The kids were all staying at the guest house at the Governor's Residence. They had done their research and had found an Australian Shepherd. We went to Uncle Bill's pet shop in Indiana, picked the puppy up, and also picked up a sweet little gray kitten that I wanted. We stopped by the guesthouse to pick up the kids the morning following the wedding to head back to D.C., and completely surprised Mike with both a new puppy and a new kitten. We showed him the gray kitten, which he knew we were getting, and then let our new puppy run loose in the house. He was totally caught off guard and was thrilled! Since all of our code names began with the letter *H*, we decided the pets needed *H* names, too. That's how Harley, our dog, and Hazel, our cat, got their names.

We brought Harley and Hazel home to the VPR on Air Force Two. Having two new pets in the VPR helped to make this feel more like home.

While I made every effort to keep our lives as normal as possible, there were some new realities that felt strange. I remember looking at our dog Harley, whose ears would perk up when we would hear the sirens of the motorcade in the distance, and say, "He's on his way home." It's also unusual to wave goodbye to your husband in the morning as he lifts off in Marine Two.

My busy days in D.C. were now filled with meetings at my office in the Eisenhower Executive Office Building, events at the Vice President's Residence, formal gatherings at the White House, and travel to support my initiatives and the administration, all while still trying to maintain some normalcy as a family.

And wouldn't you know, we actually had an additional move while Mike was VP. The entire Vice President's Residence needed a complete overhaul of the HVAC system. So we were once again completely moved out of the VPR and into another home on the Naval Observatory property that was normally occupied by a senior officer stationed in D.C. There were usually three or four other families living within the larger gates at the observatory. I actually loved that home. It was so much more like a normal home than the official Residence. Of course, Secret Service had installed fences, barricades, and cameras everywhere, but still it seemed a little more normal. We lived there for six months, then moved back to the VPR.

Over the course of the four years, it was important to me to host many events to be good stewards of the Naval Observatory just like we had done at the Governor's Residence. Mike had several congressional dinners, working through legislation and policy. But we also made it a priority to host many military functions. We had a Thanksgiving dinner for military couples one year, and we had several military family pool parties. Those were a blast. My team always totally outdid themselves with a balloon man twisting different shapes for the kids, fabulous kid-friendly food, games, and photos with us. The spouses would try to get their military member who was deployed on the phone, and we would FaceTime them right from the side of the pool. This was always emotional for me, knowing the kids would love to be sharing this experience with their deployed parent. And of course, Harley joined in the swimming with the kids at the parties.

Harley also quickly endeared himself to the groundskeepers. He is quite the Frisbee player, and loves basketball, as well. He will join right in a game. Well, he is a Hoosier dog after all, and we Hoosiers *love* our basketball. He literally guards the ball. Mike played a basketball game with the Navy Seabees who helped with the concrete for a catering pad that we also used for basketball games. Harley was right in there trying to get the basketball. Hazel, too, became a favorite of the staff, stretching out right on top of the Residence manager's computer as Oreo had the first year we lived there, before she passed away.

Having had my own online watercolor business, I knew shortly after arriving at the Vice President's Residence that I would want to do a watercolor rendering of the beautiful Victorian home. I kept the original, but made prints as well. We framed a print for each of the former vice presidents and mailed one to each of them. We also left one at the house for Kamala and Doug when we moved out.

While we lived there, I also made a point to host several events with spouses of our top military members. These spouses were so helpful partnering with me to do what we could to enrich the family life of our military members.

We also hosted Halloween parties for Secret Service families, our staff, Air Force Two families, and others. Those were always a lot of fun. Each year, we gathered at the Residence with all of the vice presidential and second lady staff families for a picnic. These people were so hardworking, it was an opportunity for many of them to meet others who were working in different areas of the White House and get to know one another better.

The vice president's home, itself, sits on seventeen fenced acres at the Naval Observatory. The entire area consists of several buildings, including the actual observatory, which are all on seventy-two acres. The Naval Observatory was founded in 1830. It is also the official time source of the Department of Defense and sets a standard of time for the whole country. The property is recognizable in Washington, D.C., because of the large, red clock outside the gates. I painted this clock as one of the illustrations for Marlon Bundo's *A Day in the Life of the Vice President*. The observatory on the grounds is a very interesting place to visit.

One of my favorite images of God is from Psalm 8:3, which says, "When I consider your heavens, the work of your fingers, the moon and the stars which you have set in place . . ." I once had a Bible study teacher explain that God placed the stars in the sky for us to look up and see. And here we were, living right across the street from the Naval Observatory! We could go stargazing any time we wanted! In addition to our trek over to the observatory the night after the inauguration with a few friends and family who had not left town yet, we went a few other times to just stargaze or planet-gaze for an evening when we had family visiting. I remember one night taking Mike's mom, Nancy, and her husband, Basil, over to see Saturn.

Mike also invited several local students to watch the eclipse from the Naval Observatory. I was with Audrey that day, so I didn't join him. But they seemed to really enjoy this unique experience. Audrey and I experienced the eclipse from a grassy field at Yale University in New Haven, Connecticut.

Knowing that we wouldn't live in this amazing place forever, I tried to do my best to pay tribute to people in their individual roles and service during the time we spent living in the Vice President's Residence. This was my opportunity to use the position in which God had placed me to help others. My staff and I were always looking for opportunities to reach out and encourage others. We invited all of the Teachers of the Year for a reception to honor all of their amazing hard work! This was so much fun for me, being a teacher myself. However, the only one they really wanted a picture with was Marlon!!

After we were settled into the Vice President's Residence, the Indiana chapter of the World Organization of China Painters reached out to offer to do something for the Residence. As I mentioned, they had donated an entire set of wildflower dishes to the Indiana Governor's Residence, and painted individual bowls for me to use as centerpieces at my First Lady's Luncheon in Indiana. I decided it might be fun to have them paint some dessert plates for the Residence. We raised private money and purchased one hundred plates that had borders that matched the border on the Biden china. These talented artists painted two copies of every state's flower on the center of each plate. We invited the artists to a reception at the Residence and used their plates to serve them. All of them—their ages ranging from thirteen to eighty—piled into a chartered bus and made the six-hundred-mile trip. It was adorable watching them search through the stack to find the plate they had painted so they could use their own. It was a privilege to be able to honor them. (I do miss those beautiful plates!)

Having been a political spouse for many years in differing roles,

I knew my time as second lady would come to an end and these were just some of the ways we tried to use the home for good. It was important to me to find ways to serve others in this role, and I learned a lot in the process.

I also spent the time making some updates to the Residence in order to care for the property. One change we made to the house was installing glass sliding doors at the top of the stairs leading to the private quarters. This allowed for a little more privacy since people are always downstairs on the main floor, not to mention it helped keep our pets upstairs. I am a very private person, and having doors to the residential area of the Residence that we could close really helped me feel like I had a space of my own. God was stretching me in new ways. We hadn't had anyone inside the Governor's Residence after hours, so having people in the house twenty-four hours a day was an adjustment, to say the least. A lot of our personal food was down in the catering kitchen in the basement where the Secret Service, doctor, and military aides were stationed twenty-four hours a day whenever Mike was at home. So if I wanted to go down in my sweats and T-shirt to get some ice cream at 10 p.m., our freezer was way at the end of the basement hallway. So it was a parade of "Hi! How are you tonight? Everything okay? Just me . . . just getting some ice cream." Not to mention the feeling of *Don't judge me . . . yes, I need ice cream at 10 p.m.*

Another project we took on with gusto was redoing the pool-house, which smelled very musty, and it had been through a lot of wear-and-tear. It was seriously due for an overhaul. We decided to raise private money and make it more of a guesthouse. It reminded me of the renovation I had overseen of Aynes House in Indiana when I was first lady. I remember thinking, *Here we go again.* But I had learned a lot in that process, so I was ready for the challenge.

The Second Family typically contributes china to the Residence. One of our projects was to frame a sample of each Second Family's china and hang this display in the dining room. At the time we lost the 2020 election, I had not designed my second lady china. I quickly got to work designing the pieces that would represent our family, and the china arrived right before we left the Residence. I don't think we even ate one meal from those plates, so I personally purchased an additional twelve place settings to take with me.

While the Naval Observatory does have four bedrooms on the third floor, there is no elevator to assist any guest who might struggle to climb all of those stairs. So we updated the kitchen and bathroom of the poolhouse, added a bedroom, and changed the location of the door, allowing a small area for a little table looking out onto the pool area where guests could have a meal. We raised private money to make the updates to the poolhouse and I wanted to be sure I was a good steward of the funds. Even though it wasn't my personal money, I worked hard to make sure we kept to a good budget and didn't spend an exorbitant amount. We enlisted some wonderful Hoosiers to keep a very close eye on expenditures. This is a place that would be used for years to come, and we wanted to really do it right.

While we were renovating, we realized that some of the very large holly trees around the pool needed to be replaced. They were literally being held together with cords. It seemed like this might be the best time to redo the pool landscaping, since we would have construction crews there anyway, so we created a better landscaping plan that would be much easier to maintain over the years. It was a big project, but it definitely added to the usability of the pool area. Once again we were blessed by Hoosier contractors and vendors who helped keep a project on budget.

The Residence was a beautiful place for me to host Senate spouses, especially since Mike was the president of the Senate. After the poolhouse renovation was completed, I had them over for a lovely poolside luncheon, and several teas. The Congressional Club was always eager to partner with me for a service project. I had become an advocate for Comfort Crew, an organization that assembled kits for children who had a parent deployed. This organization was started by Ronda Englander, who has since passed away. Ronda started this organization to help military kids who have a parent deployed. Having experienced that herself, she knew how difficult that could be. The Congressional Club bused their members to the Residence, and we assembled five hundred Comfort Crew kits. I had the privilege of personally delivering a hundred of these kits to children at Fort Carson.

These Congressional Club members were always willing to support worthy causes to make a difference. We all put politics aside and got to know spouses on both sides of the aisle better, coming together for a mutual cause.

Sometimes when God calls us to a particular position, we just don't feel adequate. Maybe the people with whom we will need to associate intimidate us, or we just don't feel prepared. Whatever the reason we feel hesitant to accept the challenge, I've found God has helped me in those situations by providing a key to the puzzle or some type of support system.

As second lady, I was required to attend many, many functions. Some were casual, some professional, and some formal. I really didn't have the means to purchase designer gowns or tailored suits that my role required. My staff and our legal team did some research to see if there was a way to have designers provide gowns for events that I could borrow. It became pretty complicated, so I decided to do what any other woman in my shoes (so to speak) would do. I signed up for Rent the Runway, which is a service that provides designer clothes for rent at a very reasonable price. Let's face it, for most of us, we would wear the same outfit for several occasions if we knew we would be seeing different attendees. I mean why not? If you have an outfit you love and you can wear it multiple times, I'm all about that! But everything I wore was scrutinized. And critiqued. I needed an economical way to be able to dress for the part. I had begun to receive several comments about how people liked my hair long. The interesting thing is . . . I had found a great hairstylist in Indiana when I was first lady. So I only wanted to use her going forward. Once you find someone who does exactly what you ask him or her to do, you never want to use anyone else. My hairstylist, Elise Barrett, occasionally would come to D.C., and when she did, she would cut or color my hair at the Vice President's Residence. But there was never really a moment when I decided to let my hair grow. It was just the fact that sometimes it was several weeks before I could get to Indiana or she could get to D.C. So it naturally got longer. Then I decided I liked it, and it has been long ever since. It was and still is amazing to me how many people comment on my hair length.

I remember one White House event where there were comments about Karen Pence's new look. This was also surprising to me—because I had pulled a gown from my closet that I had worn years before at an event in Chicago when I was first lady of Indiana. It was a long black jersey knit dress with tiny rhinestones all around the collar and down the front. That gown cost less than two hundred dollars when it was new. And I pulled my hair back off of one ear with a sparkly barrette I had in the drawer. Don't get me wrong, I loved seeing the beautiful designer gowns that the other ladies were wearing; I just couldn't afford them. I had a friend whose mother had a beautiful wardrobe. She brought several items over one day, including a designer gown that was all sequins. She gave it to me to keep, but I needed to have a seamstress hem it and alter the sleeves. Again . . . for two hundred dollars, I had a designer gown. Another friend had been in a senior position as a military spouse. She loaned me several of her gowns when Mike was in Congress that got me through formal events during those years like the White House Congressional Christmas Ball. For my very first White House Ball during Mike's first year in Congress, I had purchased a basic black sleeveless gown. That dress got me through so many formal events because I just changed the jacket or shawl to switch it up. My staff also was using Rent the Runway, because they needed to accompany me to so many of these speeches and events and luncheons and dinners. We would check ahead of time to make sure we weren't wearing the same rented outfits. I do remember seeing others at some of the White House functions in dresses I had rented for a previous event. But fortunately, I was never in the situation where I was wearing the same outfit as someone else at the White House. There were a few times in my life where that did happen, though, and when it did, I always confronted the situation head-on, asking the other woman to get a photo with me because we both had such good taste!

This new lifestyle had some unique and unexpected challenges, as did living at the VPR. Upstairs at the VPR, there is a very small kitchen. Although the NEAs all enjoyed cooking, and they would use the catering kitchen in the basement, over time we realized that cooking our own meals could be one area of life that stayed normal for us. The NEAs would frequently throw together a salad and maybe grill several chicken breasts, but then we could improvise and create our own meal upstairs in our kitchen. At the end of each month, they provided me with a bill for all of our personal food, and I wrote a check to cover those expenses. They were amazing with family brunches, and they all made a mean omelet! Some of their responsibilities included maintaining and packing the vice president's clothes and being in charge of his food. They are not responsible for my clothes or my laundry or packing or my food. So during the day or on official trips or vacation or even if we went to a restaurant, it was their job to make sure he had food, and that it had been prepared safely if not prepared by them. They would pack little lunch kits with crackers and cheese and carrots and hummus, and they always had a thermos of fresh coffee and hazelnut creamer. These were dedicated men and women who literally traveled the world with us.

By Christmas 2017, I again realized Christmas decorating fell to me. While this was an unexpected task when I was first lady, now I knew that this would be my job. I didn't know it at the time, but being first lady of Indiana had prepared me to decorate the Naval Observatory for Christmas. Many people enjoy decorating for Christmas, but for some reason it's always a challenge for me even in my own home, so you can imagine how I felt about decorating on this scale. There really isn't any part of it that I enjoy.

I don't like the planning, the details, the search for just the right decoration, or the actual decorating itself. But here is where God gave me an amazing staff, a staff that relished every aspect of decorating each year. They came up with fabulous themes, they worked with a local florist, and they commandeered wonderful volunteers. Here we would be hosting a minimum of fifteen parties each year. Fifteen parties! At the Vice President's Residence, I chose a different theme each year and always started planning for Christmas in June. The first year, we chose the theme "Make the Season Bright." We had huge stars hanging down the staircase opening. Ornaments were gold, silver, and copper. We also decided the first year to have a gingerbread house replica of the Vice President's Residence, a tradition we continued all four years. We would decorate a long tented portico area for guests to enter the house after checking their coats. As they stepped up onto the large Victorian wraparound porch they were directed to an area where they could sign a Christmas card to our servicemen and -women at a table manned by a volunteer from the Red Cross. All guests would then be announced and proceed into the sunroom for an official photo with Mike and me before heading into the house for a reception. That first year, the tree in the sunroom was a patriotic tree with ornaments contributed by military families. The house truly seemed magical during the holiday season. We always lit a menorah to celebrate Hanukkah as well. Each year, we hosted fifteen to eighteen parties. We would invite all of the Secret Service families and the military families who supported the vice president, the Residence, and Air Force Two. Many days we would have two parties on the same day. And we continued the tradition of having a tree with multicolored lights out on the lawn in front of the house.

After the first two years, knowing how the house was absolutely jam-packed with guests, we decided to construct a tent next to the house. We discovered that previous vice presidents had done this to accommodate all of the holiday guests. That became our practice after the second year. It enabled us to invite many more people to the events. I began hosting the Congressional Club for a reception and activity, like making wreaths, and I invited the Senate spouses for a Christmas tea. The tent really helped to facilitate that. We also continued the tradition we had started at the Governor's Residence of inviting local students to light our Christmas tree on December 1, complete with Mike's reading of "The Night Before Christmas" and my reading of the Christmas story. We would have activities and treats in the tent after.

Our second year, we chose the theme of "The Night Before Christmas." My staff really outdid themselves, proving once again that I had picked incredible people to help me in this role. One feature everyone loved was the buffet loaded with clear glass apothecary jars filled with all sorts of candies, imitating the "visions of sugarplums." We had scoops and plastic bags for guests to grab some sweets to carry with them for the evening. It was a big hit! Out front by the portico, we had a huge page from the storybook with a big comfy chair to help guests get in the mood. That year, once all of our official parties were finished, we invited all of our extended family for Christmas as well. When it's your turn, it's important to include your family . . . out of service to them.

The next year we focused on a Victorian theme with beautiful antique ornaments and candles on the trees. We had very large red ornaments hanging down the staircase that year. The rooms seemed so elegant. Now that we had the tent as the focus for the refreshments and entertainment, we were able to decorate the dining room table to also match the theme. There is a huge fire-place in the dining room. Each year we hung theme-appropriate stockings with all of the kids' names on them. We also included our pets, Harley, Hazel, and of course Marlon Bundo.

Our fourth year featured the theme "An Old-Fashioned Christmas." We had lots of grapevine wreaths, burlap, tin, and lanterns. We had garland lit on the wrought-iron fence all the way up the drive to the house. While we had Covid to deal with that last year, we took extra precautions to protect all guests. We limited our numbers, got creative with our food service, and canceled the photo line. This year, having the tent enabled us to practice social distancing at the parties.

Decorating was quite an involved project. We enlisted a crew of talented volunteers who had applied for the opportunity months in advance and would swoop in the day after Thanksgiving, after the professional florists had set up the trees, lights, and major dec-orations. They would wrap boxes used as sample presents, deco-rate the trees with ornaments, and set out decorations, including our menorah and manger scene. Our Residence manager provided lunch and treats for everyone. Christmas music played throughout the entire time. Even though it was a lot of work, she made sure it was very festive. We were always gone that week, allowing the team free rein over the first floor. It was spectacular to return after the Thanksgiving holidays to see the transformation. We would ooh and aah all the way through the house.

Of course we always had our own little family tree with our family decorations upstairs in our personal living space. And whichever one of our kids were home would help us decorate, po-sitioning our much-used, barely held-together Christmas star at the top. It wouldn't be our tree without that wobbly star!

One large tree was donated to the Vice President's Residence each year. It was provided by the reserve grand champion tree grower as determined by the National Christmas Tree Association. This was usually a huge, beautiful, twelve-foot-tall tree. I would try to be home to meet the grower with their loaded trailer as it arrived, but if I couldn't be there, Harley would step in for me. He loved getting involved by jumping up on the flatbed and trying to help. I think he thought the tree was for him! It was very special having real trees at the Residence. We have fond memories of cutting down our annual Christmas tree with the kids. After Mike became a congressman, we switched to artificial trees since we would be going back to Indiana for Christmas. So we had a tree in Washington and a tree in Indiana.

We had spent time at White House Christmas events while Mike was in Congress, and now we were back. One of my favorite pictures of our kids is of them at a White House Christmas Open House when they were seven, eight, and ten years old. In one of them, the girls are playing under the White House dining room table in their velvet Christmas dresses with other congressional children. Going to this event had been a tradition we tried to do each year with the kids when Mike was in Congress. They loved going to see the decorations. So it was especially sweet in 2020 to have both Charlotte and Audrey take their in-laws to a White House Christmas party and tell that story.

Each year as second lady, I painted a watercolor to be used as our Christmas card. Again, I was painting the Christmas card during the summer after we chose our theme, but it was really something I enjoyed. The first year was the Vice President's Residence in snow. The next was a watercolor of the fireplace with all of the stockings hung. The third year was of the front door with a wreath. The final was of a sleigh in the snow with a Christmas tree in it. We took the image from the watercolor and used it to create an ornament that we gave each of our guests. We also tried to have gifts for the children attending the parties. We had backpacks, puzzles of Harley with the vice president, vice president yo-yos, and water bottles. My staff totally got into the Christmas spirit. They were Santa's elves from June to December. We always had a manger scene and menorah included in the decorations.

When we left the VPR, the ornaments and decorations had all been bought by the Republican National Committee, so they wouldn't be staying at the house. I took all the ornaments with me, and my friend who had helped decorate the Indiana Statehouse and I and my former Indiana staff donated them to decorate several trees at a residential program "focused on the healing journey of women overcoming sex trafficking and sexual exploitation." We also used the decorations at a neonatal intensive care unit and several local churches. It seemed a fitting way to let these beautiful ornaments be used for a higher purpose.

It was a privilege living at this amazing Residence. So many people contribute daily to its workings. It keeps running through each successive administration because of the dedicated people.

I had learned a lot as someone who was given the privilege and responsibility of living in the home for a period of time. It wasn't going to be my home forever; that's the beautiful thing about our country. For a time, it was our place to live and to care for, and I wanted to do that well. But all of the people who work there taught me something, too.

Even though the home seems almost self-sufficient like a hive, it still required us to do our part, just like each successive colony of bees.

We all had to work together to keep it going and it mattered how we conducted ourselves, even with one another, even with the frustrations that any house brings with it.

In the end, I knew we had been good stewards of this beautiful home, that we had served its visitors and employees well, that we had honored God.

CHAPTER FOURTEEN

VPR Bees

There can be 30,000–60,000 bees in a colony.

Once we were settled into the Vice President's Residence, one of my first questions was, "Is there a beehive?" The White House had one, so I was surprised the VPR did not. I knew then what one of my first tasks would be. Having started a successful beehive at the Indiana Governor's Residence four years earlier, I was eager to get our beehive started at the VPR. My second lady staff and the in-house Residence staff were excited as well. Once again, God had prepared me for this.

We got to work and looked for a local beekeeper who would help us establish the hive. For the unveiling, on June 6, 2017, we invited Sonny Perdue, the secretary of agriculture, to attend. Our local beekeeper also regularly came to check on the hive. He showed us how to extract the honey when it was ready. For the first harvest, we invited CNN to come watch. We had purchased little tiny honey bear containers and created little stickers of a watercolor painting I had done of the VPR to go on each bear. The stickers said, "Vice President's BEES." I would go on to do several interviews with CNN and the *Washington Times* at our hive, educating the public about how they can support the bees in their area—what they can plant to sustain the bees and how they can even set out a bowl of water with rocks in it for the bees to get a drink. CNN did several pieces on the bees, even showing us harvesting the honey for the first time. While we struggled to get press for my other initiatives, the bees were always popular!

Beekeeping wasn't always easy. Like public service, there is a lot more that goes on behind the scenes than people might realize. There are also setbacks and times when adjustments have to be made that might be unexpected.

At the end of the first year, we were preparing to harvest again when we learned that our hive had been attacked by yellow jackets. They had stolen the honey and killed all the bees. Obviously the Secret Service hadn't done their job . . . *just kidding*. But this attack intrigued our groundskeeper, Derrick Williams, and he started researching hives. He even started some hives of his own on his property. As we regrouped and decided to start again the next spring, he came to me and asked if he could be in charge of the new hive completely. I was thrilled! He adapted the entrance to the hive to minimize future yellow jacket attacks. Our landscaper also ramped up our pollinator garden for the bees to do their work.

The beehive was a perfect addition. We would host children at the Residence to come to learn all about bees, see the pollinator plants, and share in some of the spoils. We would invite kids to join us for crafts, honey treats, and games and to plant their own flowers to take home to help their own bees. There is a great tree

swing at the Residence, and at some of these events, children would
sit on blankets in the yard, and I would sit in the swing and read to
them about some interesting bee facts.

I could see how God had prepared me for this role by putting
the love of teaching and interacting with children in my heart from
a young age.

I had no idea when I was teaching shop in Indiana or had my
own class of second graders that one day I would be swinging on
a swing at the Vice President's Residence teaching elementary-age
kids about bees, but even then, as a young teacher, God was teaching me these skills.

My interest in bees wasn't limited to our hive. The bees allowed
us some very interesting excursions both at home and abroad.
During my time as second lady, my staff and I visited beehives all
over the world. Every place I visited, I learned something about
bees. The practices of beekeeping vary. In the same way that cul-
tures are unique and different—and reflect different traditions of
people—so, too, are the different methods of beekeeping unique.
Everywhere I went, I was more amazed at all the details God had
included when creating the bees. Watching them work and learning about them still fascinates me.

Seeing these bees and beekeeping methods from around the
world influenced our own hive. While traveling and trying different kinds of honey, I learned I loved white clover honey the best.
So our landscaper, Kerry Duax, planted a whole section of white
clover at the Residence. At the Canadian ambassador's home, I
loved how their hives have a picket fence around them and a sign,
which inspired me to do the same at ours. We now have a lovely

white picket fence around our bees with a sign saying, "Vice President's Bees." In Canada, I visited Gees Bees Honey. They let me take a spoonful of honey right from a frame they pulled out of a hive. Talk about fresh! In Montenegro, the early hives were hollowed tree trunks. The visit there was amazing. The first lady of Montenegro treated me to a variety of "honey treats." She even gifted me one of the early hollowed trunk beehives with a plaque reading, "Montenegro hive. Second Lady Karen Pence." I love it. It had a prominent place in my second lady office . . . always a conversation starter, and I have it now at my home in my garden in Indiana.

In Lemoore, California, I had just enough time to schedule a visit to the Island District Honey Company. They had rows and rows of hives. They owned 9,200 hives in the Central Valley, including 112 hives right at Naval Air Station Lemoore.

In Dublin, Ireland, we visited Phoenix Park's beehives. They have twenty-nine hives with about sixty thousand bees in each one. The park is loaded with pollinator flowers!

On that same foreign trip, we spent a few days in London and I visited the beehive at the home of the U.S. ambassador. In the city, we stopped by a hive located on the downtown rooftop of St. Ermin's Hotel to highlight the popularity of urban beekeeping in London. My staff and I were given a real treat in California when we visited the Carmel Honey Company. We met its CEO, Jake, who was only seventeen years old and still in high school. His family-run shop in Carmel has lovely gifts and an area where you can look through a window and watch the live bees at work. He prepared special tasting pairings for us, with different food samples paired with different-flavored honey. Honey changes its flavor depending on what flowers the bees use to make it. I have recommended his store to anyone who visits Carmel. We also visited the "Bee Experience" while we were there. We walked down a lovely path that meanders past flowers and hives and leads back to the pavilion where the head beekeeper, Marc, shared with us all of his products. What an "experience" indeed! In North Dakota, we watched as the team at Dietzler Apiary harvested frame after frame of honey.

In America, the art of beekeeping is often used in veterans' therapies. It's fascinating how working with the bees can have a calming and therapeutic effect. With Secretary of Veterans Affairs Robert Wilkie, I visited Forever Heart Farm in Pennsylvania. They have a veteran beekeeping program that teaches our vets who are struggling with post-traumatic stress disorder (PTSD) how to transition back into civilian life by working with bees. The vets train with a beekeeper, then begin to have responsibility for their own hive. These soldiers who are now private citizens are part of a team, yet in charge of their own hive. The bees have a calming effect, too, on anyone who works with them. I visited a similar program sponsored by Michigan State University called Heroes to Hives. The program provides beekeeping courses and trains veterans as they overcome mental health issues.

Each time I learned something new about bees, I was reminded of how amazing God is. Each worker bee makes the hexagonally shaped cells of the honeycomb at a very slight slant to prevent the larvae or honey, whatever the cell is being used to store, from sliding out. Every. Single. Bee. I was astounded when I learned that. How amazing is God, if every single bee knows how to make the cells in the honeycomb slanted? If He is watching out for that minuscule detail, He surely can give me the grace to be able to serve

Him wherever He leads me, wherever I'm called, and I can take comfort in knowing He is completely aware of every detail of my days. If He is calling me, or you, to serve or to step up, He knows what he is asking of us, and He will give you and me the grace to handle it. Just like the bees, my work is meaningful and important, however mundane or ordinary, however spectacular and amazing. Like the bees, in my role as second lady, God was giving me long days full of purpose.

CHAPTER FIFTEEN

Launching My Art Therapy Initiative

*Over the course of its lifetime, a single bee will make
just about one-twelfth of a teaspoon of honey.*

In November 2016, I found myself in Trump Tower in New York, sitting on a couch with Melania Trump, discussing what I might choose for my initiative as second lady of the United States. She shared with me that she was going to be starting with one singular initiative, one cause. I contemplated what my one issue could be that I would champion and elevate, but in my heart, I knew right away that it would be the fascinating profession of art therapy, which I had championed as first lady of Indiana and worked on as a congressional spouse.

Art therapy is not arts and crafts. It is one of the most misunderstood therapies available today, but one of the most promising, especially for our veterans with post-traumatic stress disorder.

According to the American Art Therapy Association, "Art Therapy is an integrative mental health and human services profession that enriches the lives of individuals, families, and communities through active art-making, creative process, applied psychological theory, and human experience within a psychotherapeutic relationship."*

Again, art therapy is not arts and crafts.

Art therapists are master's- and doctorate-level trained therapists who use art to promote healing. For art therapy to occur, it has three components. It takes the involvement of the client, the therapist, and the art.

It was during my time as first lady of Indiana, from 2013 to 2017, that I became aware of how art therapy can benefit veterans. Juliet King, who was an art therapy professor at Herron School of Art & Design in Indianapolis at the time, invited me to observe Combat Paper, a program started by Drew Cameron.

I watched as veterans cut their uniforms—pieces of clothing that had contributed to their very identity for many years—into small pieces of fabric. These fabric pieces then went into a machine called a Hollander beater, which transforms the fibers into pulp, which is then made into thick paper. The vets were then invited to use stencils and paint to create something "new" onto their paper.

Some veterans don't want their fibers mixed with anyone else's. Some veterans come with other veterans in their own families, two and three generations, and make their pulp a mixture of the fibers representing many generations of service. Some want

---

* "About the American Art Therapy Association," American Art Therapy Association, https://arttherapy.org/about/#:~:text=DEFINITION%20OF%20ART%20THERAPY,experience%20within%20a%20psychotherapeutic%20relationship.

their fibers included with the fibers of other participating service members.

I watched as this transformation was taking place. I could see that healing was occurring, new beginnings happening.

I turned to the member of my security detail who was standing next to me.

"Do you know what we're looking at here?" I asked.

He shook his head, so I explained the process to him. Being a former soldier himself, I watched as his eyes, ever so slightly, became moist. He visibly took an interest as he watched with me the process unfold.

Later, in Los Angeles, I met a Vietnam vet who had had a difficult life after returning from the war, and had even been homeless. He shared with me that until he engaged in an art therapy program, he had carried the guilt of being the one who survived, but in the art therapy program at New Directions for Veterans, he learned to use art to honor his buddies whom he had lost. He had a smile on his face and no longer carried the guilt. He touched my heart in a unique way when he smiled and saluted my motorcade as we left the facility.

In September 2017, Mike's mom, Nancy Pence Fritsch, was visiting for a few days and I asked if she would like to accompany me to the National Museum of Health and Medicine. We viewed several pieces by veterans, and it was particularly special because the vets explained their work to us in person. I remember one man explaining that he had created a box that had the names inside of all of his friends he had lost in combat. It was a visual reminder of the pain he had been carrying. But he explained that he was able to close the box and contain the pain. It had been so helpful to him. Another vet showed us a very vivid piece of clay that looked like forms coming out of the artwork. He explained that once he began working with the clay, he was able to tell his art therapist, "That's it . . . that's my nightmare." It was then that they could begin working through the feelings associated with the trauma.

In Tampa, Florida, I was able to visit the James A. Haley Veterans' Hospital. While I was there, I spent some time with a veteran who gave me two of his paintings. They were beautiful landscapes. His mother explained that once he was able to start painting, he had a completely new outlook. Other vets working on leather in the pain management program of the hospital shared that while they are working on their leather projects, their pain is minimal. The artmaking process actually seems to distract them enough that they don't feel their pain on such an intense level.

As I researched how to structure my initiative, I was learning more and more about how the brain works, how it can change, and how those suffering from trauma can get relief. We visited the National Intrepid Center of Excellence (NICoE), a program duplicated all across the country at several military hospitals, where we could observe, along with other cutting-edge therapies, the incorporation of art therapy in short-term, four-week intensive sessions for our injured soldiers. One therapy incorporates mask-making, which has been featured in several national periodicals, such as *National Geographic*.

Mask-making involves the soldier using his or her own white plaster mask and transforming it into their own personal mask. They create the masks with images that have perhaps been haunting them. These masks are moving and can be distressing to see. They include tears, images of substance abuse, nails, blood, terrors, right alongside smiles and symbols of hope and cries for help. They are informative to the people who observe them, but more importantly they are healing for the vets. Once these "nightmares" are an actual visible, tangible object, they become easier for our vets to discuss. One art therapist once told me that the verbal side of the brain is the side injured in trauma, so it can be difficult for our veterans to talk about what they have experienced in combat. This disconnect can lead to problems at home once they return from duty because they don't understand why they can't talk about their trauma.

In San Diego, I had the opportunity to spend some time at the Veterans Art Project, or VetArt, which is an arts organization that helps veterans, military service members, and their dependents, spouses, and caregivers. I was especially excited to visit Julio and his wife, Rosie, both veterans, who were helped by the organization. Julio was an artist and had a small spray-art T-shirt business before he started receiving services from VetArt. Rosie had been trying to encourage him to get back into the spray-art business, but he had resisted. Knowing I was coming to visit, Julio got out his supplies and made me a shirt, which is one of my prized possessions, knowing what it represented to him—a new beginning, a fresh start, a return to who he had been. Everybody in the studio was moved by this transformation in Julio. The art therapist, Jill Brenegan, showed me around the rest of the studio, and I enjoyed hearing from the other vets about the significance of the mosaics they were creating. These were very complex pieces of art that had been carefully thought through and planned out to express who they really are. Some of them were as small as a garden stepping-stone, and some of them were quite large. A few of the veterans had created several pieces around a central theme significant to them.

I was learning the benefits could truly be for anyone. It can be very helpful for people coping with all sorts of trauma. I traveled to Japan in September 2015. My staff and I, as well as my interpreter, were invited to observe and even participate in a group art therapy session in Tokyo for women who had been victims of domestic violence. Our art therapist gave us very simple directives, like drawing something that makes us happy. She carefully continued to elaborate on our instructions, helping us to go deeper and analyze for ourselves why we had chosen to draw what we had. At the end of the session, I asked my interpreter what she thought of the experience. I have quoted her many times over the years. She said, "My heart feels clean!" That truly summed up the evening.

Art therapy has been used to help people who have experienced unimaginable things. In New York City, I had the privilege of visiting with the art therapist who had helped victims of the 9/11 attack. She was able to show me the progression of the artwork illustrating a change in her clients' perspectives. The images were haunting at first, dark and vividly portraying some of the tragedy. But as the healing process progressed, colors began to appear in the artwork, and hopeful images replaced the haunting ones.

I had once been told by an art therapist that clay can be a very effective medium because there is nothing between the client and the art. In other words, there is no pencil, no paintbrush. It is just the clay in the client's hands. After Hurricane Maria in October 2017, I visited Puerto Rico. I had seen how veterans experiencing PTSD had worked with clay and observed how their hands miraculously created the nightmare they were internally dealing with but had not been able to describe in words. Therefore, I knew clay could be very beneficial to children who were experiencing the trauma of Hurricane Maria. I had my staff reach out to the art therapist in Puerto Rico to see what supplies we could bring with us. I suggested clay, and she was very enthusiastic. Having been an art teacher in the Washington, D.C., area, I reached out to my former clay supplier and purchased all of the air-dry clay he had in stock. We delivered the clay to the art therapist who was set up in a makeshift art studio. She already had traumatized children working at several art stations, and she was very grateful for our small contribution. Very few of the kids even looked up to notice us. She had them engaged in the creative process, and we were witnessing how beneficial immediate help can be.

As first lady, serving on the board of the Riley Children's Foundation had allowed me to continue to support and advocate for the art therapy program at Riley. The art therapists knew I was 100 percent behind everything they were doing. As second lady, I was invited to do syringe art with the patients they were supporting. They had just opened the new art therapy room, which I was thrilled to see. I had participated in syringe art once before when I was first lady. The process involves loading paint into a syringe and squirting the paint at will onto a white paper or canvas. The idea is to take something (a syringe) that is normally intimidating or frightening . . . and change the perception. We had a blast! Once we finished, I took out a large, long-sleeved white shirt and rolled it over the multicolored paint-splattered paper. Then I had all of the kids sign their names on my shirt. That is one of my favorite shirts to this day!

Once I had decided this would be my initiative, it was time to start planning how this would work. My second lady of the United States (or SLOTUS) staff's first assignment, having never heard of art therapy, was to learn everything they could about it. We reached out to Judy Rubin, who is recognized by most art therapists as one of the most influential art therapists in the United States. She had also been the "Art Lady" on *Mr. Rogers' Neighborhood* for three years. Judy sent us videos to watch and helped to educate us about the history of the profession. Many credit England as the place where art therapy originated. The term was first coined by the British artist Adrian Hill in 1942, but art therapy was growing in America and Europe at the same time. American art therapy pioneers Edith Kramer and Margaret Naumburg were working to develop art therapy in the U.S. in the 1940s.

We also met with Dr. Thomas DeGraba, who is continuing to do extensive research at Walter Reed National Military Medical Center on the physical, measurable benefits of music and art therapy. Dr. DeGraba shared research with me. While I certainly didn't understand all of it, I did understand that art therapy, including music therapy, was making a real difference for these veterans. And I could see it for myself.

Whenever my staff and I tagged along on one of the trips Mike was taking as vice president, we would arrange to visit art therapy programs and universities offering art therapy as a major. We soon became fairly knowledgeable about art therapy, and I wanted to make a difference by spreading the news.

Finally, in 2017, I launched "Healing with the HeART."

This initiative was threefold. It was aimed at 1) raising awareness for the profession of art therapy, 2) encouraging young people to choose this profession, and 3) letting people know that art therapy can be for anyone who has experienced trauma. We launched the initiative at Florida State University on October 18, 2017. I would go on to witness art therapy in Belgium, South Korea, Germany, the United Kingdom, Indonesia, Japan, Australia, Estonia, Georgia, Colombia, Egypt, Israel, Argentina, Chile, Poland, Panama, Puerto Rico, Florida, Texas, New York, Hawaii, Washington, D.C., California, Arizona, Michigan, Pennsylvania, Ohio, Virginia, Nebraska, Alaska, Massachusetts, Montana, and Indiana.

We designed some special bracelets to give to art therapists we visited around the world. The bracelets were silver with a flag, the Great Seal of the United States with my signature on the back and an art charm that might be an easel, a palette, or a paintbrush. We just wanted to leave them with something that showed we appreciated them. What we were learning was that there needed to be more art therapy programs offered on the university level so that more students could pursue this major in colleges around the world. That was one reason we wanted to launch the initiative at a university.

Now we were off and running, trying to visit as many art therapy programs as possible.

Our visit to the INECO Foundation in Argentina, the Institute of Cognitive Neurology, was very informative. Art therapist Clara had created a display that showed the healing progression of one of her clients, Maria. Maria had suffered a stroke at age twenty. It wasn't until nine years later that she began receiving therapy from Clara. Over the course of two years, we could see Maria's progression exhibited through the artwork. She had made several self-portraits. Originally Maria couldn't make any connection between her thoughts and emotions. Clara explained how Maria's abilities improved over time as she attended therapy, including her use of line, texture, and color. I met with Maria personally, and she shared that art therapy is a tool for people who suffer, and it has been a lifesaver for her. Maria's story motivated me to be as proactive as I could be to encourage people to seek help through art therapy. The difference it made in Maria's life is staggering!

Art pieces that clients create in art therapy can be expressions of a healing journey. In Poland, I met with several art therapists. One of them, Anita, presented me with a blue rocking horse, about twelve inches in height. She explained that she uses it in several different circumstances. Because the rocking horse moves, it symbolizes to the client (who makes his or her own rocking horse) the idea of always moving, and reinforces the notion that you can't sit still in life.

Art therapy is practiced in countries around the world, and it's been amazing for me to be able to witness it and be a small part of getting these programs the attention and support they deserve. On one of our official trips to Asia when Mike was vice president, our daughters, Charlotte and Audrey, were able to accompany us. My staff, daughters, and I joined the first art therapy session with children at St. Luke's International Hospital in Tokyo. Afterward, we had a vigorous discussion with several art therapists, one of whom was the art therapist I had met years before as first lady of Indiana. She was the one who conducted the session where afterward my interpreter had said, "My heart is clean." Art therapy was growing in Japan, and a few years later, I had the privilege to announce a $55,000 grant from the U.S. embassy in Tokyo to support a pilot art therapy program at the University of Tsukuba. This was the first opportunity Japanese students had to pursue art therapy without leaving their country. I just recently heard from Cheryl Okubo, this same art therapist who conducted this pilot program. She is preparing to host the first conference for professional art therapists in Japan. And she wanted to thank me for my work to advance art therapy and make the Japanese program possible.

During an Asia-Pacific trip in April 2017, we celebrated Easter with service members in Seoul, South Korea, toured the Sensoji Temple in Tokyo, learned the art of flower arranging, ikebana, and learned batik in Indonesia as well as visiting key landmarks in Japan and Australia. But during this trip, we also were able to include an art therapy discussion in Jakarta, Indonesia, and learn about the profession of art therapy in Australia. In each place we visited we developed a better understanding of the need for and the different uses of art therapy.

On our way back to D.C. from our Asian trip, we stopped to refuel in Hawaii. I visited the U.S. Army's Schofield Barracks on Oahu and heard soldiers share with me how the art therapy program there had saved their marriages and ultimately saved their lives. One soldier said, "I don't go to that dark place anymore." Two of the gentlemen showed me paintings of couples with a sunset behind them. Another shared with me how clay had been very effective for him, and even though he was not a licensed art therapist, he had started a clay program at the local art museum for veterans and their families.

The stories the art therapists shared were always so meaningful to me. They of course were intimately acquainted with the struggles behind the artwork, and the progress their clients had made. Each piece always has a story behind it, and once the art therapist describes the piece, it becomes very clear to see what it represents. In Europe I was given a tour of an art therapy display in Tbilisi, Georgia, where there were several varied pieces of artwork, including paintings and sculptures. There was one piece in particular that resembled a musical score made of metal rising from a pile of sand, showing how music had helped the individual to rebuild his life from the ground up. It was immensely inspiring.

One of the most beautiful experiences my staff and I will remember for many years was our visit to Instituto Teletón in Santiago, Chile. These young people have many physical challenges—some with no hands—and yet they create beautiful art, and they share the joy in creating. One young girl presented me with her artwork to take with me. It was a very bright and colorful image of many animals on a brilliant patchwork background. I told her how much I loved it and that I intended to hang it in my office at the White House. She was so moved that she started to cry. It was a lovely moment for both of us.

I did have one art therapy client whom I connected with on a personal level and got to know. While I was first lady of Indiana, I attended a board meeting at Riley Hospital for Children. There was a presentation by a young girl named Emma, who explained to us the difficult journey she had traveled after being diagnosed with a brain tumor. She had many, many surgeries that affected her ability to read and even function at times. But her attitude was amazing. I followed her out of the board meeting into the hall. I had to meet her! We connected, and her mother stayed in touch with me as her medical condition changed over the years. Emma reached out to me and made me aware that she had started a program at the hospital called "Emma's Art Cart." She wanted other patients at Riley and all over the United States to also have access to art supplies because her art was a real help to her during her treatments. Later, she was nominated for the Jefferson Awards for her art kit project. We encouraged everyone we knew to vote for Emma, and she won! She came to D.C. to receive her award at the gala, and I invited her and her family to lunch at the Vice President's Residence. I followed up with the Congressional Club, inviting them to the Vice President's Residence to help me assemble Emma's Art Kits to be shipped to hospitals in their congressional districts. And once again, these amazing spouses showed up! Emma is now employed at Riley, helping others who struggle with trauma.

One thing I have learned along this journey is that sometimes I encounter thoughtful, appreciative people who are grateful for what I have done. And sometimes, I am met with criticism or misunderstanding. But one thing to remember is that I am not doing these things for the accolades. Mike likes to frequently use a Ronald Reagan quote, "There is no limit to what you can accomplish if you don't care who gets the credit." Our pastor used to remind us we were working for an "Audience of One." Just an aside as you eagerly jump in where God is calling you. Your new calling is usually something that stretches you, takes a lot of energy and time, and comes with few worldly rewards.

However, I do want to mention a wonderful woman who truly used her position to benefit others. Rima Al-Sabah is the wife of the former Kuwaiti ambassador to the United States. Each year she would host a gala where she recognized someone who was working for a particular cause, and she would use the gala to highlight them. The proceeds from the gala always went to a U.S. charity. One year she recognized me, and it gave me the opportunity to speak about Tracy's Kids.

Another amazing woman in this regard was Louise Linton, the wife of Treasury Secretary Steven Mnuchin. Louise hosted two fundraisers in her home to raise money exclusively for Tracy's Kids. She did this completely selflessly because she felt such a heart for the art therapists and the children at Tracy's Kids.

I spent a lot of time hearing from enlisted soldiers and how they struggle with the trauma of the military, but they're not the only ones. Officers suffer, too. At Naval Medical Center Portsmouth in Virginia, I was honored to hear an officer share his journey with art therapy. He realized he had been putting on a strong façade for years, but inside he was struggling. He told me he had mistakenly assumed he had to just keep it together for those in his command. But then he realized that by getting help himself, he was actually paving the way for his soldiers to be vulnerable and get the help they needed as well. Many times we expect so much of our military families without giving them the help they need.

Visiting the United Kingdom, I met with British soldiers who had fought years ago, but were receiving the benefits from art therapy now. Art therapy really began in England . . . so it was especially meaningful for me to visit there. I visited art therapist Jan Lobban, who works at Combat Stress, an organization that offers services for veterans dealing with mental health problems. Jan had arranged for three veterans and one spouse to share their art and art therapy experiences. Richard, one of the vets, explained that art therapy is like a telephone line. It helps him communicate. He doesn't have to go through the left brain like he would need to in "talk therapy." He shared that he had been angry for years. But after his art therapy, he has learned to cope better and control his anger. His wife, Joan, said she has seen a significant difference in her husband because of art therapy, adding that things are a lot better now, and Richard is more confident than he used to be and much easier to live with. His artwork showed images of someone very angry, but he was able to get all of those feelings out. It reminded me of a story that an art therapist who worked with children with cancer had shared with me years before. A young child she worked with came into the art therapy room and created some pretty dark images. At the end of the session, the child left the artwork on the table. The art therapist asked if the child wanted to take the art with her, and she explained, "No. It will make my mom cry."

Robert, another client in London, shared that through art therapy, he has found a love for art and is even building an art room. His art therapy experiences have helped him significantly with anger issues. Robert had two pieces of artwork that had been hanging in his bedroom that he gifted to me. To have a client part with something so meaningful to them, something that represents their healing journey, meant so much. We hung those pictures in my second lady office and they always reminded me not only of the trauma of combat, but of the healing power of art therapy.

While art therapy is effective for veterans and people suffering from illnesses, it can help with so much more. At Bellevue Hospital in New York, I learned how effective art therapy can be for addiction. It really can help anyone dealing with trauma.

In Israel, I was fascinated to learn that they have over three thousand art therapists, with many in their elementary schools. They truly understand the value of art therapy.

I availed myself of every opportunity to share and learn about art therapy. In January 2018, I gave a presentation on art therapy to the Conference of Mayors held in Washington, D.C. I'm glad to see so many of our cities here in the U.S. providing more and more opportunities for art therapy. In Texas, I visited diverse programs from Fort Hood, to San Antonio, to Fort Worth, to Dallas, to Austin.

In Munich, the art therapist I met with showed me little puppets they use with their clients; in Phoenix, Arizona, they have several art therapy centers called "PSA Art Awakenings." A client presented me with one of her pieces, and it still hangs in my home office today.

One interesting aspect of art therapy is something that art therapists say all the time: you don't need to be an artist. Each client uses the art materials to create something meaningful to them. In 2017, I hosted an art therapy breakfast at the Vice President's Residence for those attending the Creative Forces Creative Research Summit. A woman came up to me and gave me a small one-inch copper wire bicycle with square wheels. She said she gives these to people to explain how she felt before she received help from art therapy. The wheels wouldn't turn.

At the University of Colorado, I toured the Marcus Institute for Brain Health to learn about their cutting-edge art therapy programs for veterans.

But by far, one of my greatest experiences with an art therapy client took place in St. Petersburg, Florida. I was going to be presenting at a luncheon designed to explain the benefits of art therapy. I was seated next to Chris Stowe. He was a Marine (Oorah!) who had tried everything to improve his PTSD. He was initially not interested in art therapy at all. It is sometimes difficult for tough guys to turn to something like art for help. They frequently resist at first. Chris was able to try glassblowing. He forged new creations in the furnaces of a glassblowing oven. And it was miraculous. So miraculous that his wife said she wanted to meet the woman (Chris' art therapist) who had given her back her husband. Chris even started a workshop at a glassblowing facility at the Morean Arts Center's Operation: Art of Valor program in St. Petersburg. I took my daughter-in-law, Sarah, with me, and we both made our own glass flowers with Chris' help. Everywhere he speaks, Chris shares how art therapy saved his marriage and his life. He had literally tried everything.

Art therapy is not the only therapy out there to serve our vets. There is drama therapy, pet therapy, dance therapy, horse therapy, music therapy, and beekeeping therapy, as well as traditional therapies. There are so many ways our veterans can be served after serving our nation.

I had the privilege, while serving as ambassador to the President's Roadmap to Empower Veterans and End a National Tragedy of Suicide, PREVENTS, to witness the benefits of many of these therapies. Music therapy especially seems to help vets bring order back to chaotic thoughts. One vet in Alaska shared that before music therapy, he couldn't remember where he kept his keys or what he had just started to do. He said it felt like his thoughts were scrambled. As he progressed through music therapy, he and some other vets even started a band, and he told me he no longer struggled with simple tasks like he had before.

The scientific proof of these benefits is something I share wherever I speak. Now we can actually see the brain change on an imaging machine that uses magnetoencephalography (MEG), which measures ongoing activity in the brain on a millisecond-by-millisecond basis, displaying where activity is generated in the brain.

As Dr. DeGraba had shown us, we can measure anxiety before and after music therapy. We can measure oxygen levels at the cellular level. There is help for our amazing vets. There is help for anyone struggling, whether it be from cancer, an accident, or the aftereffects of trauma.

Since we have left office, I still hear about art therapy efforts and have learned of the impact that it has on people. Many people have shared with me that they had never heard of art therapy before. So maybe by trying to tell the stories of healing that I've witnessed, someone will reach out for the help they need.

A single bee will produce only about one-twelfth of a teaspoon of honey in its lifetime. The promotion of art therapy might be my one-twelfth of a teaspoon of honey, but if my efforts to spread awareness about this field can save or improve someone's life, I want to do all I can.

CHAPTER SIXTEEN

Second Lady Initiative: Military

During a single collection excursion, a honeybee
will go to fifty to a hundred flowers.

When speaking to military families, I would often say that while I didn't know what it was like to be a military spouse, and would never pretend that I did, I did know what it was like to have to move for your husband's job and find a new job of your own in a new city, all while trying to raise a family.

A military member may have to make what is called a permanent change of station, or PCS. While that might be an inconvenience for a military member, it can also represent a huge adjustment for the family. Children change schools, the family needs to find a new home, the spouse may need to find resources such as childcare or services for disabled children or parents. And the spouse then needs to find new employment. This can be especially difficult for spouses with professional licensing. Many states require new licenses when someone moves to their state to practice their skill. A hairdresser, a teacher, an attorney, a nurse, etc. (professions that require licenses to practice) cannot start by just looking for a position. They need to first apply for a new license, which can be very costly and time-consuming, especially if the new state requires additional education. Most states do not let individuals begin the process of applying for a professional license until they have actually moved to their new address, meaning the spouse cannot even start this huge endeavor until the move has taken place. Since the process is so time-consuming, many spouses shared with me that by the time they procured the license and began the job hunt, it was time to move once again. For these spouses who have worked so hard to attain these degrees in the first place, this can be very frustrating and expensive. Their income is usually vital to the family budget, as well.

While promoting art therapy began as my major initiative, there were so many people who wanted me to champion their cause—just like when I was first lady of Indiana. It could have been overwhelming, but God had prepared me for this, too. I felt like God was giving me another opportunity to make a real difference while I was in this position. As my time as second lady progressed, I learned more and more about the struggles military families face, and military spouses specifically. I knew that I and my staff could do more while we were in this position of leadership. It wasn't about me, or us; rather it was about lifting up others and drawing attention to important, sometimes overlooked causes while I was in this position. While we continued to do what we could to elevate art therapy, I chose to partner with organizations that support military spouses and families, too. I wanted to come alongside the people who are frequently in the background, the spouses I often call "the home-front heroes."

More and more, I was approached by people inside and outside the administration to see if I could help our military spouses. Honestly, at first I was a bit confused. As first lady of Indiana, I had been made aware that professional licensing was a huge problem for military spouses. Michelle Obama and Jill Biden had made efforts to use the spouses of governors to reach each state to try to affect licensing restrictions for military spouses, so I was very familiar with the issue. I assumed it had been solved and I knew Indiana had made strides on that topic.

Once again, God was calling me into a position and a role I hadn't known I would fill. All of the years of moving, and leaving the house we had built as a young family and thought we would retire in, had prepared me and given me empathy for our military families, who are asked to move on average every two to three years. I knew I could encourage these spouses.

I wanted to learn as much as I could about how to come alongside our military spouses, and I knew I should get advice from as many people as possible.

I invited top military spouses to the Vice President's Residence to share ideas. After all, I knew that they of all people would have the experience and know how to make changes for our military spouses.

These senior military spouses had so much wisdom and enthusiasm to share. As I subsequently spoke to spouses around the United States and world, I shared much of this enthusiasm. It can be very inspiring to hear a military spouse who has had thirty-five to forty years of experience say she is going to hate to see it end. Military spouses all belong to an exclusive club. They get it. Yes, they have struggles, but they also have friends all over the globe who have been there for them through all of the ups and downs of military service.

I was attending the annual dinner at the White House for the National Governors Association in February 2017 and was seated next to Nebraska Governor Pete Ricketts. I realized I was sitting next to Pete for a reason. God wanted me to have this discussion. I told Pete I thought the issue of military spouse licensure had been solved by Michelle Obama and Jill Biden. He explained that while they'd certainly created more awareness, nothing substantial and long-lasting was really achieved. He explained that unless there is some type of federal legislation, each new state legislature can rescind whatever progress may have been made at the state level.

This was stunning to me. I had been resisting any involvement in this issue, thinking it had been solved. I went back to my office, sat with my team, and asked them to find out exactly what needed to be done. Meanwhile, I decided to make military spouses my next major focus, while still promoting art therapy. Not being a military spouse myself, I didn't want to assume I knew which issue to prioritize. Perhaps licensing was the most urgent need, but I wanted the spouses themselves to inform me, so I began a "listening tour." I started with the USS *Ronald Reagan* while we were on a trip to Tokyo. My staff and I set up some basic parameters. We asked the posts to assemble a group of spouses at each level to meet with me. Each spouse could participate in a roundtable discussion and express their main request in two or three minutes. I explained at the outset of each meeting that I couldn't solve every issue facing military families, and I asked them each to tell me what issue they would be thrilled to have me work on. I told them I wasn't sure I could do much, but I was willing to try.

We visited spouses at Schriever Air Force Base (now Schriever Space Force Base), U.S. forces at Yokota Air Base in Japan, Marine Corps Air Station Miramar, Luke Air Force Base, Naval Air Station Joint Reserve Base Fort Worth, New York Air National Guard spouses in Syracuse, Grand Forks Air Force Base, Fort Carson, and more.

And we compiled a list.

Education, childcare, health care accessibility, and licensure seemed to surface over and over again. But it turned out that licensure was by far the top issue, so we set about to see what we could do. I launched my initiative and embarked on doing what I could to solve at least one problem for these spouses.

I wanted to use my position to elevate people who are sometimes overlooked, whose struggles don't always get told, and who are not always appreciated.

I was so inspired visiting spouses all over the country and world. I created military spouse silver charm bracelets for female spouses that had a star, a flag, and the Great Seal of the United States with my signature on the back. For the male spouses, I gave them second lady challenge coins that we had designed. They were gold with the Great Seal and had a white rim engraved with KAREN PENCE SECOND LADY OF THE UNITED STATES. According to the Department of Defense, challenge coins are "meant to instill unit pride, improve esprit de corps and reward hard work and excellence." They are shared through a handshake. The giver of the coin has one in their right hand, and as they extend their hand to shake the receiver's hand, the coin is passed off. The receiver frequently responds in kind, handing off their own coin representing their organization or military unit. Those in service just as frequently have a coin display shelf where they collect all of the coins they have received. I have a large shelf displaying all of the ones I have received over the years. They are treasured possessions. As I met each spouse personally, I shook their hand, thanked them for their service, and gave them a bracelet or coin to remember that I support them and am grateful for their sacrifices. When speaking to these spouse groups as a whole, I explained that the bracelets and coins were a way for me to say, "I see you. I appreciate you. We're behind you." I asked them to remember that fact whenever they wore the bracelet.

Encouraging military spouses and military families is one of the things I loved most about my time as second lady. Blue Star Families is an organization that works hard to support military families. They sponsor events and work to connect military families to the communities where they serve. Military OneSource is a government organization that is available to any member of the military or their family. They provide 24/7 support in any area, whether that is helping to find employment support, childcare, schools, mental health assistance, etc. What I found in my role was that sometimes I was just a mouthpiece, a spokesperson using my position to make others aware of the support out there. So sometimes, when God calls us, it might be just to share what we know.

Once word got out that I was supporting military families, opportunities to speak came flooding in. In San Antonio, I spoke to the first Military Spouse Economic Empowerment Zone. San Antonio has a huge military population. This event was supported by USAA. I participated in a roundtable discussion at the Institute for Veterans and Military Families at Syracuse University in New York. There I spoke with National Guard spouses who are often left out of the benefits that other military spouses can access.

I had the privilege of addressing spouses at Naval Station Norfolk in Virginia, Coast Guard spouses in both Maryland and Base Alameda in California, Fort Detrick in Maryland, Camp Lejeune in North Carolina, Fort Campbell in Kentucky, Grand Forks Air Force Base in North Dakota, Guam, Schriever Air Force Base in Colorado, Marine Corps Air Station Miramar in San Diego, California, Naval Air Station Joint Reserve Base in Fort Worth, and Fort Stewart-Hunter Army Airfield in Georgia, among others. And it was so special when I visited Naval Air Station Meridian in Mississippi. There I had the privilege of honoring my own daughter-in-law, Sarah, who is married to our Marine son, Michael.

Along the way, I visited military spouse businesses in order to bring awareness to the spouses who were making their dreams a reality in difficult situations. These men and women realized that perhaps the best way for them to stay employed through the many moves and struggles would be to start their own business. Many times these were businesses that spouses operated out of their homes. Other times, they were restaurants or storefront operations.

I myself had started a little business when Mike was governor, and I knew how difficult it can be to go from the creative idea to getting the product on the shelves.

This was another way that God had prepared me for this season. I hadn't known it at the time, but I was able to truly relate to the difficulties, and the drive, of starting a business. The military spouses I met carried out their business dreams with such inspiring passion.

Perhaps the most well-known military spouse business is R. Riveter. Named after the famous World War II promotional figure "Rosie the Riveter," R. Riveter was started by Cameron Cruse and Lisa Bradley to "provide mobile, flexible income to military spouses as they move across the country every 2–3 years in support of their service member." This innovative company allows military spouses to work from their home to cut specific pieces of materials that will be used back in North Carolina at the headquarters to assemble beautiful cutting-edge handbags and totes. Each bag is stamped with the individual identification numbers of the military spouse "riveters" who worked on that bag.

There were so many inspiring stories of military spouses' businesses. When I traveled to Billings, Montana, to speak with the spouses of the Montana National Guard, I first made a stop at the Sassy Biscuit. This quaint little restaurant, started by military spouse Jilan Hall-Johnson, brings southern comfort food to the Northwest. Wanting to encourage other military spouses who maybe had an idea of a business they would like to start, we partnered with the Small Business Administration during my events to connect spouses on the spot in real time with people who could help them take their dream and make it a reality. I realized I could be the conduit who connected spouses to those in the administration who could help them with the nuts and bolts of how to start a business.

In Detroit, I visited Le'Host, a beauty salon designed to be an encouragement to those dealing with hair loss. The owner, Haith Johnson, has a heart for helping all women feel beautiful.

When speaking to military spouses at Naval Air Station Lemoore in California, we took a little side trip to Board & Brush in nearby Hanford. This particular franchise business is owned by a military spouse who employs other military spouses. It was great fun! I painted a wooden sign to celebrate Audrey and Dan's wedding. Little did I know then that my other daughter, Charlotte, would marry a Navy pilot and be stationed at Lemoore! I visited another Board & Brush franchise in Virginia with two friends to make Charlotte and Henry a sign for their home when they got married.

In Charleston, South Carolina, I visited Grey Ghost Bakery, a veteran and military spouse bakery that had received assistance from the Small Business Administration, which also supported them during the Covid-19 pandemic.

Another unique military-spouse-owned business was DocTerra Mobile Veterinary Services, which is based in Vale, North Carolina, and owned by Dr. Terra Smith. It is a completely mobile vet clinic.

Many spouses also started clothing, jewelry, and baking businesses in their own homes.

I was joined by Secretary of the Air Force Barbara Barrett at Davis-Monthan Air Force Base in Tucson and Luke Air Force Base in Glendale, Arizona. What an honor to travel with her! I was joined by Secretary of Labor Eugene Scalia at Naval Air Station Jacksonville in Florida. I was helping him launch the Department of Labor's TEAMS (Transition Employment Assistance for Military Spouses). TEAMS offers online career and job search courses to assist military spouses while living on base. He and I then headed to Social Grounds, a local coffee shop owned and operated by a veteran and military spouse. Their shop is also involved in providing mental health awareness and services to veterans in their community. I kicked off the Military Spouse of the Year Town Hall. I also keynoted the Joint Military Spouse Conference in Hawaii.

In addition to these great opportunities, we made a concerted effort to speak with spouses every time we traveled with Mike.

From Warsaw, Poland, to Ottawa, Ontario, to Rome, Italy, to Yokota Air Base in Japan, to Singapore.

I have to say it was a tremendous thrill to meet with the Blue Angels and observe a flight demonstration at Naval Air Station Pensacola. The staff at NAS Pensacola met with me for a round-table discussion of military spouse and mental health programs available there.

I knew legislation was the key to correcting the licensure issues. I joined Senators Tom Cotton and Jeanne Shaheen and Representatives Susan Davis and Jim Banks as they announced legislation to improve military spouse employment opportunities. But legislation wasn't the only answer. We needed to educate and partner with businesses around the country. Twice during my time as second lady, I hosted American Corporate Partners at the White House to brainstorm ways private sector companies can address the military spouse employment issues, and I hosted Hiring Our Heroes Military Spouse Employment Working Group at the Vice President's Residence. This proved to be a great collaboration of private and public sector leaders working together on this issue. I addressed their group again in Tampa, Florida, a year later. The message I was able to convey was that military spouses are the kinds of people businesses want to hire. They are usually strong, independent, hardworking, and flexible. Many have undergraduate and graduate degrees. And they want to work.

One of my main goals was to create an awareness of the employment obstacles that military spouses face. Sometimes that meant addressing businesses and recognizing new businesses at the Military Spouse Employment Partnership that are dedicated to training and hiring military spouses. I met with veterans on this issue at the Defense Communities National Summit and spoke with military families at the Pearl Harbor Remembrance Circle, as well as Naval Special Warfare Command spouses at Naval Amphibious Base Coronado. I addressed the National Association of State Workforce Agencies (NASWA) Veterans Conference in Washington, D.C., and the American Legion Auxiliary National Convention in Indianapolis.

We hosted the National Governors Association at the Vice President's Residence, where I addressed all of the governors on this topic. I mentioned specific governors by name in my first remarks. In following years, other governors would come up to me and ask if I was going to tell the group what their state was doing. Governors are very competitive, and I used this to my advantage, always remarking on the great things being done around the country for spouse employment . . . mentioning the governors . . . yes . . . by name. I was joined by former-Governor Doug Ducey in Arizona for a roundtable discussion of how his state has been a leader in creating a universal occupational law that allows spouses to practice in Arizona using another state's license. And Arizona's law isn't just for military spouses. It is for anyone with a professional license who moves there.

We also hosted Honor Flight veterans during Public Service Recognition Week and Military Appreciation Month. Military families were celebrated at the Eisenhower Executive Office Building by getting to meet our now-famous bunny, Marlon Bundo.

I participated in a USO and Congressional Club joint event assembling five hundred care packages for spouses of deployed military service members.

I had one really fun surprise experience when the military plane I was traveling on coming back from the Summer Special Olympics

World Games in Abu Dhabi was undergoing maintenance in Shannon, Ireland. While sitting in the airport, we noticed a huge group of U.S. National Guard troops getting snacks and souvenirs in the airport. So we gathered them together and took photos and told them how proud we were. It was fun for all of us to see someone else from home.

Airports frequently provided these types of opportunities. Returning from a trip in April 2019, I was walking through Ronald Reagan National Airport when I noticed a group from the Northeast Indiana Chapter of Honor Flight. These amazing veterans had just had a very memorable day in our nation's capital and were returning home. They were in a line heading to their plane. I made a point to stop and speak to each of them, hear about their fabulous day, and take selfies and thank them for their service.

God bless our veterans. They are truly special people. While Mike was vice president, we occasionally got the call that there was going to be a "dignified transfer" at Dover Air Force Base in Delaware. This meant one or more of our treasured service members was being returned home to be buried. This was something Mike and I never turned down. We always dropped whatever else was on the schedule and headed to Dover to meet with the families and respectfully attend the dignified transfer. The ceremony began with us taking as long as was needed or wanted by the families to pay our respects to them. We would ask them about their family member, making sure they told us a favorite story or two. We would hug and cry and hold their hands. Then we would head out to the tarmac to await the family's slow and solemn arrival by bus. They would disembark the bus and sit in rows awaiting the removal of their loved one's flag-draped casket from the C-132. This is a very solemn, well-executed, respectful ceremony. Sometimes press is present if the family allows it. Many times, they don't want any press there. We all stand and salute or hold our hands over our hearts as the ceremony proceeds. The casket is loaded into a vehicle and slowly taken away. It is a heartbreaking moment. Our presence, especially having the vice president and second lady attending, is a way to honor their service and ultimate sacrifice for us. It was a privilege to do our small part to comfort these families and honor their loved ones.

In our own family, we have two military spouses, but that isn't why I chose this initiative. However, watching these two wives as their husbands have been away for long periods of time training and going on deployments has given me unique insight into the challenges and difficulties that military families face. Their strength is inspiring. Sarah gave birth to our granddaughter alone one month early while Michael was away training. A month later, Michael unexpectedly deployed for nine months. This was a deployment he was added to at the last minute. So Sarah went through much of Avery's first year on her own. And she did an amazing job! Charlotte and Henry had recently gotten married when Henry deployed. Not the most ideal way to start your marriage. But these women persevered in the face of trials common to many couples in the military.

Many spouses would share stories with me about how it seems like Murphy's law goes into effect the minute their service member deploys. The car breaks down, the air-conditioning stops working, the refrigerator goes out, the sink leaks, etc. Many times, Charlotte or Sarah would travel with me when I spoke to spouse groups. As we visited military families around the world, I hoped that by sharing our family's experiences, I could encourage others. Our pastor used to say, "Everyone is under-encouraged."

In my position, I wanted to do all I could to elevate and encourage these home-front heroes. And sometimes, the role God is calling us to is to do just that, to encourage. For many Americans who haven't grown up around the military, they may not realize the struggles military service members and their families face, but they're the ones defending our country, keeping it safe, so that we can all follow our dreams.

CHAPTER SEVENTEEN

Spreading Awareness About Mental Health

Honeybees use the sun as a directional device when departing and coming back to the hive.

During my time as second lady, I had several opportunities to bring attention to mental health, the importance of taking care of ourselves mentally, and asking for help if we need it. The coronavirus pandemic brought mental health issues to the surface in a new way as people struggled with its effects. I was able to help bring awareness to this issue, but I had also already started working in this area with our veteran population.

Veterans are an underappreciated population in our country. Before the onset of the coronavirus pandemic, I was asked to be the lead ambassador to PREVENTS, the President's Roadmap to Empower Veterans and End a National Tragedy of Suicide. The statistic is that twenty-two veterans a day commit suicide. It truly is a national tragedy. I was honored to be chosen to be a spokesperson for this amazing effort. I hosted at the VPR the entire team coordinating all of the different agencies involved in PREVENTS. I asked everyone who was there to share their role in this effort. The meeting really helped me to better understand the mission and how I could help.

Right after Covid struck, I spoke at the launch of REACH, the campaign encouraging people to reach out to others who may be struggling with mental health. This era of a global pandemic was new to all of us, and we wanted to be sure to inform the public of places they could go to get help if they were feeling the effects of the pandemic.

I was also asked to help open the national parks after the Covid shutdown was lifted, which was a true joy for me because I have always seen national parks as places that are truly majestic. Opening the parks was a way of encouraging our fellow citizens to get outside, commune with nature, and get some exercise and fresh air. People had been struggling, and one thing we were learning was that getting outside was beneficial for combating the isolation and depression experienced during the lockdowns. So drawing attention to the national parks as a haven for Americans to experience during this difficult time made perfect sense, and I was privileged to be able to share that message.

I had grown up camping in state parks and occasionally a national park. The outdoors are invigorating. I loved hiking, camping, biking, swimming, all the things that come with a weekend of camping. During our kids' "growing-up years," we took many family vacations to national parks. We really wanted our kids to experience them. It was always a lot of fun—getting around the country to experience a totally new and wide-open environment. Mike reserves the word *glorious* for moments that are truly glorious and give glory to God, and at every national park, he would say, "This is glorious." With our kids, we visited Acadia, Grand Canyon, Yosemite, Redwood, Rocky Mountain, Everglades, Yellowstone, and the Great Smoky Mountains. They have visited many more national parks now that they are grown, but these were the ones we visited as a family.

Simply being at a national park touches the soul, and I have always loved it. Mike and I had the privilege of going to Yellowstone with Secretary of the Interior David Bernhardt to highlight the administration's funding of long-overdue maintenance projects in our national parks. Mike and I helped to repair the boardwalk right in front of Old Faithful. Sure enough, right on cue, the geyser spewed forth! I also had the opportunity to visit the park's artist-in-residence. On the way to the park, Mike had the motorcade stop. He asked the entire staff to get out of their vehicles and take a moment to appreciate what they were experiencing. Many of them had never been to Yellowstone, and it was a moving moment.

The first park we opened was Great Smoky Mountains. It was raining, but we really didn't care. It was just so great to be outside, highlighting some of the great features of the park. We all walked up a long paved lane to an overlook where we had a large tent set up. We were getting completely soaked, but after having been cooped up for so long during Covid, none of us really seemed to care. It reminded me of Gene Kelly in the movie *Singin' in the Rain*. The next park we were invited to help open was Rocky Mountain. Our daughter, Charlotte, happened to be in Colorado that day, and it was her birthday, so she was able to join me along with her husband's family, for a birthday hike around one of the lakes. After the official parts of my day were over, Charlotte and I took a short detour to visit the place where Mike and I had made the decision to run for Congress back in 1999. Returning to that ranch was especially meaningful to me. So many years later, here we were, in a completely different position but still trying to listen to God's call on our lives every day, still trying to do it all with "no flapping." God had truly blessed us for being willing to just make ourselves available to what His plan was for us.

Another national park, not far from Washington, D.C., is Shenandoah. I made a point to drive out to visit it as the park employees safely reopened the park. I took a long hike with the park employees and really enjoyed it. Each time we visited a national park, we made a point to do as much social media as we could to get the message out that the parks were open again. I remember standing by a rushing stream or under a canopy of majestic trees or at the edge of a lake with mountains behind me, with a lapel microphone clipped to my collar and my staff holding a small screen with script for me to read while I recorded into their phone. We had so much fun being out in nature and trying to capture that feeling on our short videos that we posted. If people could sense the wonder and joy and relaxed spirit that I had as I taped these encouraging messages, perhaps they would venture out to experience the benefit that being outdoors brings.

On National Arbor Day in April of that year, 2020, Mike and I attended a ceremony on the South Lawn of the White House. The president spontaneously called on me for a few remarks. I wasn't expecting it, but I seized the opportunity to share a few words about mental health. I made a point to look right at the press and say, "It's okay to say you're not okay." We wanted people to ask for help.

The entire nation was suffering from the effects of the pandemic, and loneliness, depression, and substance abuse were increasingly becoming a struggle for so many people. These were issues our veterans were already struggling with—before the pandemic even started, we had a national crisis of veteran suicides. So in addition to opening the parks, I made a concerted effort to visit as many veterans hospitals as I could. I wanted to highlight the great programs they were offering. So much had improved in our veterans hospitals over the past four years, and I wanted to encourage our vets to reach out for help.

It was meaningful for me to be able to assist in the efforts to promote mental health during the pandemic and to encourage the people who had been dedicating their lives and service to help others. There are so many devoted individuals who answer the suicide hotline and stay on the line as they help those struggling walk inside the door to get help. Many of them shared personal stories and a lot of them have been there themselves, so they understand exactly what the caller is feeling. I wanted to do all I could to bring awareness for our veterans and others to have access to the suicide hotline, especially the new "988," that they could call. And our Veterans Affairs hospitals were implementing so many new programs they could utilize as well.

Drawing attention to our national parks and their dedicated employees, especially during a pandemic, was truly a special moment for me. Our national park rangers, like the rest of the nation, had been through some tough struggles during the pandemic. At each park, we took time to laud them and their efforts and encourage them. With fewer visitors to the parks, these workers became isolated and lost some of their sense of purpose. As the shutdown ended, they were playing a big role in helping our nation to overcome some of our mental health issues, and I always reminded them that they were truly on the front lines. Coming back to visit the parks as second lady brought back so many memories from our visits when our kids were small, and I hoped my fellow Americans would take advantage of the National Park System to create their own memories and to restore their mental health.

It was during these efforts that I was also made aware of the "Walking Marine," Terry Sharpe, who annually walks from North Carolina to Washington, D.C., to bring awareness to the cause of preventing veteran suicide. In 2020, I joined him for the last leg of his walk. We walked from the Washington Monument to the White House. What he didn't know was that we had arranged for him to walk through a crowd cheering and the Marine Band playing right up to the steps of the White House on the South Lawn to meet President Trump and Secretary of Veterans Affairs Robert Wilkie. Terry was totally overwhelmed. It was a great way to thank him for everything he was doing. He was one of those people who stepped up, took the challenge, and made a difference . . . when it was his turn.

The National Suicide Hotline, if you or someone you love needs help, is 800-273-8255. You can also just dial 988.

CHAPTER EIGHTEEN

Trips

During their six- to eight-week life span, a worker bee will travel one and a half times the circumference of planet Earth.

Imagine training diligently over several months or even years to participate in the Winter Olympics. Your sport is skiing. You are going to travel to Austria to represent your country. You arrive and are so excited for this moment to finally be here. You head to your competition to find that it is freezing rain. There is very little snow. How do you react?

Well, if you are anything like me, you would be very disappointed and discouraged. Probably in a pretty bad mood. But those are not the reactions I witnessed when I traveled to Austria to lead a presidential delegation to the Special Olympics World Games. These young men and women were thrilled to be there, and still very excited to participate despite the conditions. It was moving to witness their optimism and enthusiasm. It was contagious. Our delegation was very small, and we didn't stay more than a few days.

I wasn't sure exactly what to expect. This was my first time leading a presidential delegation. But the enthusiasm of the participants and the hard work of so many volunteers truly inspired me. I think it took our whole delegation off guard. I was used to people wanting to speak to me because there was something I could offer them, something I could do for them. But these young men and women were just happy to see us. They wanted to tell us all about their accomplishments, introduce us to their teammates, and explain their sport.

Our delegation included Eugene Young, U.S. chargé d'affaires ad interim to Austria; Charles Glazer, special advisor to the transition, U.S. Department of State; Katherine Henderson, special assistant to the president for presidential personnel; Crissy Haslam, first lady of Tennessee; Loretta Claiborne, former Special Olympics athlete; and my friend Jane Wainwright from Indiana. We all were invited to participate in the closing ceremonies.

Again, it was freezing rain. But we watched as athlete after athlete, from 110 countries, entered the arena with their hands raised high, wearing clear plastic parkas over their country's apparel to keep them dry. The weather had absolutely no effect on the high spirits of these young people. Music was playing, arms were swaying, athletes were hugging each other, and our entire delegation was in tears watching and being drawn into their excitement and realizing the privilege we were experiencing just by being there. It was probably the highlight of my four years as second lady. It was such a pure showing of camaraderie and excitement, a culmination of years of hard work. I was encouraged, myself, to see their resilience, their high spirits. It was a good reminder to me to focus not on everyday struggles, but to instead take joy in every moment as these athletes did. There was no way these athletes were going to let the weather dampen their moment. They didn't see the struggles of a challenge; they saw the possibilities.

I gave each of the athletes a little note with a copy of one of my watercolors, *Cardinal in Snow*, to help them remember this special winter experience.

This was truly one of the most inspiring experiences of my time in public life. So imagine my excitement two years later to be asked once again to lead a delegation this time to the Summer Special Olympics World Games. In addition to the other guests invited, including Linda McMahon, administrator of the Small Business Administration; Steven Bondy, chargé d'affaires ad interim, U.S. Embassy Abu Dhabi; Dr. Jerome Adams, surgeon general of the United States; Mariano Rivera, cochair of the President's Council on Sports, Fitness, and Nutrition, former pitcher for the New York Yankees, and 2019 inductee to the Baseball Hall of Fame, and his son, Jafet; I took along my daughter Audrey. These games were held in Abu Dhabi. We had much more lead time for this event, so we designed a special second lady challenge coin to give to each of the athletes.

Our first stop was the soccer game between Kenya and the U.S. team, which took place at the Zayed Sports City before the opening ceremonies. I was asked to do the coin toss with a Eunice Kennedy Shriver commemorative coin. Audrey and I and the entire delegation had so much fun watching the soccer match with members of the U.S. Bowling Team. They were big cheerleaders for their fellow athletes. They were very talkative and wanted to share so much about themselves and their teammates and their individual sports.

For these games, we had the honor of participating in the opening ceremonies. The night of the opening parade of athletes from around the world, we arrived at the venue early. The American athletes were all lining up in their respective sports groups. As I got closer, a young man recognized me and linked his arm with mine and decided to escort me around to the groups. It was a special moment. As we met with each group, it was a sort of reunion. Some who had also competed in the Winter Games two years before remembered the cardinal painting, and were eager to talk to me about the sport in which they would be competing. As the time drew near for us to head out into the arena, I assured them I would be at as many competitions as I could. We led them out, proud once again to be able to support this amazing group of individuals. This was an amazing memory to share with Audrey.

We attended a myriad of competitions, from outdoor soccer to gymnastics to weight lifting.

During our time in Abu Dhabi, we also wanted to recognize the role Sister Cities International (SCI) plays in promoting citizen diplomacy one individual, one community at a time. Since 1956, SCI has worked to create global relationships based on cultural, educational, information, and trade exchanges.

As second lady, I was asked to be the honorary vice chair of SCI. My time working with the organization as first lady of Indiana was especially meaningful, and now I was able to serve on another level.

Whenever we traveled outside the country we tried to connect a city in the U.S. with their sister city overseas just like we had done when serving Indiana. Abu Dhabi's sister city was Houston, so we participated in a brief tour of the Founder's Memorial. There is an amazing sculpture featured there, *The Constellation*, that is made of wire and lights that replicate a three-dimensional portrait of Sheikh Zayed, the founding father of the United Arab Emirates. Then, on behalf of the mayor of Houston, I presented Abu Dhabi with a letter and a gift of a framed postcard featuring the "First

Manned Moon Landing." In exchange, Falah Al Ahbabi, chairman of the Abu Dhabi Urban Planning Council, presented me with a three-dimensional sculpture also titled *The Constellation*, a smaller version of the memorial sculpture, which I then took back home with me and presented to Houston City Council member Jack Christie at NASA's Johnson Space Center. Our entire delegation was invited back to the palace where we were greeted with amazing hospitality and a plethora of food, as is the custom. This was a special moment of being able to represent the United States abroad.

These Sister Cities International mini-exchanges always were inspiring to me. It was so satisfying to hear citizens of a foreign country speak so highly of cities in the U.S. where they had built memories and relationships as they learned more about our culture.

Other Sister Cities exchanges occurred in Chiba City, Japan, with students from the Youth Ambassador Exchange, a tree planting in Brasilia, Brazil, and a gift exchange with the mayor of Quito, Ecuador, to highlight Quito's relationship with Coral Gables, Florida.

Back at the Special Olympics complex, we toured the area dedicated to health screenings for the athletes. Through Special Olympics, athletes are screened for issues they may have with their vision, hearing, bone density, feet, teeth, etc. Many volunteers donate countless hours for these screenings in addition to all the volunteer hours involved in coaching these athletes. Again, individuals step up and answer the call to serve when it's their turn.

As we headed home after an amazing trip to the Special Olympics World Games, the entire delegation was inspired, to say the least. It had been so much fun to see the athletes get so excited to see Linda McMahon and talk with her about WWE, World Wrestling Entertainment. She was quite the celebrity in the weightlifting arena. The athletes also wanted pictures with baseball legend

Mariano Rivera. These were precious moments and sweet memories. I felt privileged to be a part of this celebration.

The trips to the Special Olympics were unique trips abroad because the office of the second lady does not have access to a plane. For these two presidential delegations, we were provided military transport. Usually we traveled commercially, being very careful with our budget to make the most of the resources we had to promote my initiatives, but my team also became very creative incorporating some of my initiatives as we traveled with the vice president and his team.

Many times, those joint trips included official second lady events as well. For example, in February 2017, Charlotte traveled with us to Belgium. She and I took a side trip to Flanders Field American Cemetery to pay our respects to American servicemen killed during World War I. On many of these trips, I had the privilege of meeting with the first ladies of these countries. I remember the first lady of Montenegro, Nata Markovic, guiding me on a boat ride of Lake Skadar before showing me Montenegro's beehives.

One of the challenges we all faced in the second lady office was staying focused on our agenda, our initiatives. There were always current events, crises, distractions swirling around, just as there are in your own life. I mean, let's face it, responding to the twittersphere alone could have been a full-time job. But we just didn't let those issues distract us from our mission. As first lady and second lady, I had a very short window of time to make a difference. There were definitely crises that our office did need to respond to with the vice president. These were moments where I accompanied Mike to places where we knew our presence could be a comfort.

They involved not only natural disasters, including hurricanes, floods, and volcanic eruptions, such as the one in Guatemala, but also tragedies involving shootings. These were the moments where I knew God was giving me His strength to comfort those feeling an indescribable loss. We visited those in the hospital after the Sutherland Springs, Texas, church shooting. It was a humbling moment when one of the victims asked if he could pray for us. That is a moment I will never forget. Visiting Las Vegas after the Mandalay Bay shooting, seeing the crosses all lined up on the street, each one with a name of an innocent victim, was shocking. This was so senseless. We also visited the Chabad of Poway synagogue in Poway, California, near San Diego. We spoke with those who had been present during the shooting. In those times, God's calling is clear. Our job was to show up, to be there for those left behind, to listen, to console as best we could. Being used by Him to comfort is humbling. Most of us never feel quite adequate in this type of tragedy, but I still wanted to go, to be there, to provide whatever consolation I could.

Part of being vice president and second lady is always being available to head to any crisis to offer support. These visits were always heartbreaking. We heard tragic stories from families who fled the Maduro regime in Venezuela. We had an opportunity to meet with them at a church where they were receiving shelter and aid in Manaus, Brazil. They shared how there was no food in Venezuela, that they would get up at 4 a.m. to go stand in line in hopes of receiving a loaf of bread.

We headed to Guatemala after the eruption of Volcán de Fuego in June 2018. Mike had been scheduled to take a Black Hawk helicopter to survey the damage and meet with displaced families near the site, but his schedule changed, and he ended up having to stay at the airport for a meeting, so I went with the first lady of Guatemala instead. We reached out to every family in the camp. We listened, we hugged, we cried.

We also took trips to remember global tragedies such as the Holocaust. We went to Yad Vashem, the Holocaust museum in Jerusalem, and visited Birkenau and Auschwitz in Poland with Prime Minister Andrzej Duda and his wife, Agata Kornhauser-Duda. It is important to never forget this atrocity.

It was such an honor to be at Joint Base Pearl Harbor–Hickam to receive home the remains of our American soldiers who fought in the Korean War. Mike's dad was a Korean War veteran, so this trip was especially personal for us. We invited two people who had lost their fathers in that war to accompany us: Diana Brown San-filippo, whose father was shot down over North Korea when she was four, and Rick Downes, who was only three when his father left for war. It was an emotional day.

For Thanksgiving in 2019, we decided to surprise the troops in Baghdad. It wasn't easy slipping away without most of my staff knowing, but it was so special to surprise the servicemen and -women and take a moment to visit with them. Serving them their Thanksgiving meal was truly an honor. Mike and I had frequently served somewhere over the Thanksgiving holiday, whether it was in Indiana or at a military base, when we were visiting our son or having military families to the Vice President's Residence.

On one of our Asia trips, we traveled to Singapore. My staff and I headed out to a site about an hour away to visit with military spouses. It was a delightful outside venue. Like all visits with military spouses, it was a great opportunity to encourage them and thank them for all of their sacrifices. The next morning we had a breakfast added late to our schedule with the prime minister's wife, Ho Ching, in their home. She had been so gracious after chatting with me about issues I cared about that she assembled several guests who shared my interest in the healing power of art, especially with children. I was so touched by her thoughtfulness.

There were other trips, such as Cairns, Australia; Papua, New Guinea; and others. Each time I felt humbled to be representing my country on an international stage.

Our last overseas trip occurred right before Covid hit. We traveled to Jerusalem and Rome. During that time, our daughter-in-law, Sarah, was staying with us since she and our son were in between moving from South Carolina to Arizona. It was great having her along and being able to show her the Holy Land and having the privilege of meeting Pope Francis. It would have been better, of course, to have Michael with us, too, but getting foreign leave while you are in the military is very difficult. Due to our very busy schedule in Israel, we compressed a tour of Jerusalem into about three hours. Walking where Jesus walked, seeing the sights we read about in the Bible, makes the Bible come alive. I wanted my staff and Sarah to experience as much as we could in that short window of time. Once again, I wanted to make the most of a great opportunity.

CHAPTER NINETEEN

Children Getting Married

*A phenomenon called swarming happens when a colony
has gotten too big for its current hive and is getting ready
to split into two or more new hives that are smaller.*

One of the things that has always been important to me is maintaining our family in the midst of a very busy political career. God has helped me to be able to keep the important things "important," to not let our family get lost in the mix. My son, Michael, gave me a nickname once he had entered the military and engraved it on a silver bracelet. I proudly wear the title, "Mama Platoon Sergeant." Having a busy and robust family life just meant we had to be organized and totally plugged in to Mike's schedule. All three of our children got married between the 2016 and 2020 elections, so it was a busy and joyful time in the Pence family. I have always tried to maintain a great line of communication between Mike's current scheduler and me. These women really have had to keep a lot of plates spinning, and they have always respected our family time.

And so, scheduling weddings during this busiest time of our lives, while challenging, was not impossible.

Michael and Sarah met at Purdue University. They dated through college and were dating seriously while Michael went to Officer Candidates School in Quantico, Virginia. After completing OCS, Michael went to The Basic School for the Marine Corps and received a flight commission that took him to Pensacola, Florida. Sarah was visiting him there in April 2016 when Michael proposed to her during sunset on the beach. We knew it was happening that night, and all of us were waiting upstairs at the Governor's Residence for the call. As soon as they told us she'd said yes (we didn't doubt it!), I was filled with an amazing supernatural love for Sarah. She was the first to marry into our family, and I had always wondered what that would feel like. It felt amazing! When you hear someone say yes to marrying your child, it's this wonderful assurance of knowing your child has someone who will be walking their life journey with them. It was the greatest feeling!

We all loved Brown County State Park in southern Indiana and had so many great memories from our stays at the governor's cabin, Aynes House, where we had spent so much time. Sarah's mom and stepdad also loved to vacation there in the park's cabins. So Michael and Sarah decided to have an October wedding at the lodge in the park. In the fall, southern Indiana is breathtaking, with its rolling hills covered with beautiful fall foliage. There is a beautiful outside area at the lodge with an arbor, and the lodge itself has a great room for wedding receptions.

Michael was already stationed at Naval Air Station Meridian in Mississippi, continuing his training as a Marine pilot. He and Sarah decided that it would be best for them to go ahead and get married that December, and Sarah could be with him in Meridian instead of waiting until October, but they still planned to have a big October wedding the following year. We learned that this is actually pretty common in the military. Many times young couples will get married at a small ceremony before a deployment or military move.

Sarah and her mom and I looked all over Indianapolis for a suitable venue for a small, intimate wedding. After looking at many options, Michael and Sarah came to the conclusion that the Governor's Residence would be the perfect place. We had a lovely winding staircase that Sarah could walk down and a large room for the dinner after. It was one of the most beautiful weddings! Michael had asked me to hold Sarah's wedding ring, and Mike said a prayer at the wedding. While December 28, 2016, was the day they became man and wife, they only had immediate family, grandparents, and their best man and maid and mate of honor attend. We had had a small rehearsal dinner at a restaurant a few nights before. They saved many of the traditional activities, like toasts, dances, bouquet toss, etc. for the large wedding that they still intended to have in Brown County in October to include all of our family and friends.

In October 2017, we traveled from Washington, D.C., to celebrate Michael and Sarah's wedding in Indiana. It was so much fun! We finally got to have a huge rehearsal dinner the night before with lots of toasts and celebrating. Their wedding was amazing, with the sword ceremony performed by Michael's Marine Corps friends. The weather was spectacular, so they were able to use the beautiful outdoor venue. We celebrated late into the evening, and stayed in cabins at the lodge . . . Secret Service and all. The next day, Mike's brother, Greg Pence, who is also a Marine, and his wife, Denise, hosted everyone at their nearby home for a spectacular brunch.

Like Michael and Sarah at Purdue, Audrey and Dan had dated

through college at Northeastern University. They were in their last semester at Northeastern, when we had made plans to meet Dan's parents at dinner before Audrey and Dan's graduation. While we were finishing up an Asian trip with a refueling stop and a visit to Schofield Barracks in Hawaii, where both of our daughters accompanied us, Audrey got a phone call that Dan and his father had been in a private plane crash. Audrey had chatted with Dan earlier that day before we headed to Schofield Barracks, and he had mentioned that he was going to go with his dad while his dad practiced some takeoffs and landings. We hurried back to Air Force Two and took off, not knowing the condition of Dan or his dad. It was a long nine-hour flight back to D.C. We got Audrey a reservation to fly straight to Connecticut as soon as we landed. She spent several weeks with Dan in the hospital as he recuperated. Tragically, Dan's father did not survive the accident. Neither Audrey nor Dan attended graduation. Dan went on to have a complete recovery after weeks of being in the hospital.

By February 2019, Audrey was now at Yale Law School, and Dan was working in D.C. Dan proposed on a beach in Cape Cod where his father had regularly flown his family during his childhood. It started to pour down rain as he proposed, and we have the most spectacular photo of the wind blowing Audrey's long hair as Dan lifts her off her feet right after she said yes. The whole day we had all been watching the weather. We knew the proposal was coming. Mike and I were in Germany, and we kept texting Michael to track the weather with his pilot apps to see if Dan would get the proposal in before the rain. It turned out Audrey and Dan both loved the fact that it was raining!

Audrey had always wanted a destination wedding. She didn't want all of the fanfare that a D.C. wedding would bring with her dad being the vice president. But the rules for flying Air Force

Two overseas for a personal wedding were very restrictive. So Italy's Amalfi Coast was off. When Audrey was accompanying me on a trip to Abu Dhabi to represent the United States at the Special Olympics Summer Games, she spent the whole flight researching the possibility of doing her wedding in Hawaii. A friend had suggested the Hawaiian island of Kauai. By the time Audrey chatted with me about the details, she had already found a great venue. She hadn't remembered at that moment, but Mike and I had taken the kids to Kauai for our twenty-fifth anniversary vow renewal. I thought the idea was spectacular! With Michael in the military, stationed in Arizona by then, she knew Hawaii would be a destination to which he could most likely arrange leave. She and Dan set a date in May 2020, arranged for us to rent out the entire facility due to security issues with Mike being vice president, and started making plans.

But like many other couples during the past few years, they had to postpone their wedding due to Covid. Hawaii was locked down. They checked with the venue for any future dates available and chose a date in August that was actually Dan's parents' anniversary. We moved forward with changing flights, rental homes, rehearsal dinner plans, etc. And again it was postponed due to Covid. By now there were not many dates available. Audrey and Dan chose July 3, 2021. Being a holiday weekend, they knew Michael and Henry had a better chance of asking for leave.

By the time of Mike's vice presidential debate in October 2020, Audrey and Dan were becoming weary of postponing their wedding over and over. They reached out to us and said they had decided they wanted to go ahead and get married less than two weeks later in a small ceremony on November 1, two days before the election. They knew Michael and Sarah would be in Washington for the election; Mike's mom , Nancy Pence Fritsch, and her husband,

Basil, could be there; and Charlotte (now married herself with her husband, Henry, deployed) would be there election night as well. Dan's family could drive in from Connecticut. They informed all of us of their plans, and we all were immediately on board.

Yes, it was a busy week, but these two young people were our priority. That's one of the things we have always tried to accomplish: making our kids and our family a priority. With our busy schedules, it would be very easy to put our public life first, but by the grace of God, we have tried the best we can to let them know they come before anything else in our careers. So after jumping through many hoops to get their license and to be able to get married on the sidewalk in front of the D.C. courthouse, with family there and friends tuning in through a live stream, Audrey and Dan got married! Mike performed the ceremony, with Audrey legally signing the marriage certificate as officiant. Audrey and Dan asked me to say a prayer at the celebration dinner that evening, and I asked Mike's mom to help me draft it. We celebrated with a small intimate wedding dinner with them, saving many of their traditions for their July wedding, as Michael and Sarah had a few years before.

Their July wedding was flawless. After much waiting and planning and replanning and more replanning, they had an amazing celebration. Audrey and Dan asked me to say a prayer at the Hawaii wedding as well, so I shared the same prayer I had said at their first wedding. One part of the prayer included an Irish blessing, "May the sun shine warm upon your face; the rains fall soft upon your fields, And until we meet again, may God hold you in the palm of His hand." Right then, a sprinkling of rain fell and a rainbow appeared. It was incredible to see it all come together after so much time. Throughout the setbacks and difficulties, Audrey and Dan had made the best of the situation and celebrating them was so special. The ceremony was very moving, the reception was magical, and the only disappointment was that Michael had been unexpectedly deployed in May, shortly after the birth of his daughter, Avery. We were so grateful Michael had been at the actual wedding in November, but he was missed in July. At four months old, Avery did a fantastic job carrying the rings on a little ribbon that her mom, Sarah, had tied around them. Audrey and Dan were so grateful to everyone who kept rescheduling their own travel plans to attend. They planned many amazing adventures for everyone, including a spectacular rehearsal dinner cruise hosted by Dan's mom, snorkeling, hiking, Audrey's bridal shower luncheon, and a brunch the morning after. Audrey said at her reception to everyone how even though they were officially married in November, they wanted to establish the foundation of their marriage with family and friends who are the ones who have supported them through the years and would continue to. It was a beautiful weekend!

At Michael and Sarah's October wedding, Henry Bond, one of Michael and Sarah's friends from flight school, attended. He and Charlotte met at the wedding, but they didn't really get to know each other. Almost a year later, Henry called Charlotte out of the blue. Michael had been telling Henry how much Henry reminded him of Charlotte. At that time, Charlotte had been working in Los Angeles but was headed to Harvard to pursue her master of theological studies degree. Henry went to see her in July 2018, on her last weekend in Los Angeles. They started dating long-distance, and each made an effort to see the other as often as they could. Months later, we were all on pins and needles waiting for the call that Henry had proposed. He, too, chose a beach for his proposal. So all three of our kids got engaged on the beach!

They got engaged in July 2019 and had to wait several months before setting a date because of Henry's military situation. Eventually, they decided on a December 28, 2019, wedding—coincidentally the same anniversary as Michael and Sarah. Henry had attended the U.S. Naval Academy, and they wanted to be married at the chapel there. Annapolis, Maryland, was—and still is—a special place for them. Henry's parents hosted a beautiful rehearsal dinner at the Naval Academy. Since Annapolis is about forty-five minutes from Washington, D.C., the Vice President's Residence seemed a perfect place to have the reception. After the wedding ceremony at the Naval Academy chapel, we all headed back to D.C. for the reception. It was very festive with lots of dancing and celebrating. The next day, Mike and I hosted a brunch for out-of-town guests at the Residence. Charlotte and Henry headed to California, where they were stationed. Henry deployed that same April on a lengthy deployment on the USS *Nimitz*, where he was away from home for almost a year.

Some second families have planted trees on the Naval Observatory property in the past to mark their time there. So we decided to commemorate Charlotte and Henry's wedding by planting a serviceberry tree in October near the spot where the wedding reception tent had been. For their wedding reception, they had used berries from a serviceberry tree in their centerpieces since it was a Christmastime wedding. We also planted a redbud tree from our whole family that will mark our time there for generations to come. Alongside our family tree, there is a plaque that reads:

The redbud tree, which grows in many woods across the state of Indiana, was planted by Vice President Mike Pence, Second Lady Karen Pence and their family. "But blessed is the one who trusts in the Lord, whose confidence is in Him. They will

be like a tree planted by the water that sends out its roots by the stream. It does not fear when heat comes; its leaves are always green. It has no worries in a year of drought and never fails to bear fruit." Jeremiah 17:7–8
Naval Observatory, October 4, 2020

There is a small garden on the property at the Vice President's Residence, installed by the Bidens, with a small white arbor at its entrance. Inside, there are large slate stones on the ground that encircle a sweet little fountain. The whole area is quite small, but intimate, surrounded by waist-high shrubs. Each Second Family chooses one stone and engraves on it the names of all of the family members who were in the immediate family while that particular vice president served. We were very pleased that all of our kids and their spouses' names are engraved on our family's stone. Even though it wasn't easy having five weddings between the 2016 election and the 2020 election, it was truly a blessing to be able to celebrate all of these weddings and now marriages.

We are continuing the tradition of planting trees at our new home in Indiana. As each new grandbaby is born, we plant a tree for them on our property with their name next to it. That is their tree, and they can watch it grow as they grow.

CHAPTER TWENTY

Her Bees Will Stay

*Bees can identify human faces with their
own "facial recognition software."*

Once again, in 2020, we found ourselves on the campaign trail. Although there were still rallies on this campaign, there were fewer due to Covid. I remember many evenings heading over to the campaign office to sit in front of a monitor and host several Zoom fundraisers in a sitting. My team and I also headed out on our own to campaign, but not as often due to the pandemic. We had campaigned a lot in 2018 and 2019, but this year, I limited our in-person events. Still, I wanted to do whatever I could on the campaign. I always felt it was part of my responsibility to do what I could for the cause, for the team. I saw my campaign appearances as an opportunity to speak about faith, family, and freedom.

The vice presidential debate took place in Utah and was a lot of fun. Once again, we were all together except for Henry, who was deployed. That week, before we left, Michael and Sarah had surprised us with the great news that we were going to be grandparents! This was super exciting for everyone. I literally started screaming when they told us. We were having dinner outside by the VPR pool, and luckily the Secret Service didn't come rushing in when they heard me. Our family was growing, and even in the midst of everything going on with Covid and the election, we were going to be grandparents. We were thrilled.

Even more exciting changes were coming. It was also the week after the debate that Audrey and Dan made the decision to get married on the Sunday before the election. The last days of the campaign were definitely busy times for our family, but full of joy.

For election night, we decided to watch the returns from Mike's vice presidential office in the White House. We had Audrey and Dan (back from a very short honeymoon), Michael and Sarah, and Charlotte. We had learned our lesson four years earlier, and this time we took food and drinks with us, knowing this could go into the wee hours once again.

As history has recorded, this election conclusion went on and on and on. I really didn't think we would lose. I felt like we had more to do and the administration was just getting started, not to mention all of the initiatives that my team had been working on. It was a busy time and I was focused on the holidays coming up, especially Christmas. Friends had very graciously allowed us to stay in their home in Vail, Colorado, for Christmas, which would bring our family together for the holidays. I remember Audrey and Dan diligently watching the returns and keeping me informed as I reserved lift tickets, organized our ski gear, planned menus, and wrapped presents.

We of course had lost two elections before. This was the first election we had lost since we had kids. It was such an about-face for me. I really did not think we were going to lose. I hadn't really prepared for a loss. But again, I needed to trust God with all of it. All of a sudden, though, our future was a huge unknown. Perhaps now more than any time in the past, I had to totally surrender and trust that God had a plan and knew what was best for us. We went ahead with our Vail Christmas, and our amazing kids gave us a beautiful scrapbook and collage of their favorite memories of the past four years. They encouraged us so much, focusing us on this new chapter in our marriage, in our lives, reminding us we had been through so many changes in the past, and we would be fine.

By the time I realized we actually had lost, I needed to purchase a car and find a home in Indiana. On a more immediate front, I needed to find a rental home in the Northern Virginia area for the next few months to allow me to finish the school year where I was teaching art, and for Mike to finish his work in Washington at the transition office, which each vice president does for the six months following the inauguration.

Even though we didn't know what the future was going to hold, we would still have one another and be together as a family. With God's help, we had worked hard to prioritize our family and we knew that no matter what happened, we would all still be close and connected.

In a way, those final days of our past chapter of service were the same as life had been before. For twenty years of public life, our kids have been right there beside us.

Now we were coming up on Mike's last official duty at the United States Capitol, where we had started creating memories when our kids were five, six, and seven years old. We had shared taco dinners on the steps, gone to July Fourth concerts, brought our kids' friends to the top of the Capitol dome for birthday parties, attended funerals of presidents, swearings-in, and countless votes. Our kids each served as Senate pages, and we had greeted so many constituents at the Capitol, and attended many State of the Union speeches.

So it was fitting that in these final hours, on January 6, 2021, our kids were still right there with us. On that day, Charlotte and I had decided to go to the Capitol with Mike. We wanted to do so more out of a sense of nostalgia, with it being Mike's last official duty after so many memories in this storied place. Our motorcade had actually taken an alternate route to the Capitol that day, right past Audrey's apartment, where she was working from home. Our family has a tradition that whenever we part ways, we make a circle with our fingers and thumb that we hold out until we see the person who is leaving centered in the middle of it. This symbolizes a circle of God's protection of angels surrounding them and keeping them safe. Audrey heard the sirens and stepped out onto her balcony. She sent us a video of the motorcade passing through her fingers and thumb making a circle.

Charlotte was with us in person since she was visiting us at the time while Henry was deployed. As news reports have shared so many times, the two of us, along with Mike's brother, Congressman Greg Pence, who was sitting with us, were ushered out of the Senate gallery by Secret Service to join Mike in his ceremonial Senate office right off the Senate floor. Audrey and Michael checked in with us by phone to make sure we were okay, and they kept checking in as the day and night progressed. In those hours, I was experiencing how God truly had carried my family as a father carries his son.

Our kids had been raised to revere this seat of our nation's government. Thanks to God's immeasurable grace, our family had stayed together over the years of change, challenge, and lots of transitions. Michael, Charlotte, and Audrey had traveled this journey as well. This was part of their tapestry, and it hadn't been easy for them. The evening of January 6, as Congress was preparing to reconvene, all of our kids were speaking with their dad, encouraging him, supporting him. They helped Mike as he crafted his final remarks for the reconvening on the Senate floor once the lawmakers were back in the Capitol to finish their duties. Our children's support was a sweet and beautiful thing to experience. Through all of the struggles and turmoil, the sacrifices and stress, God had blessed us. And thanks to the Secret Service, Capitol Police, and federal and local law enforcement, the violence was quelled, and the work was completed. As tragic as that day was, I was witnessing the grace that I hadn't forfeited because I had been willing to let go of the comfortable, the safe, the steady to follow God's calling so many years before.

The next morning, we began packing again and preparing to leave the Vice President's Residence. I reflected back on that verse I had thought of so many years ago, Jonah 2:8. We held on to it in our very first campaign, and it will always be a comfort to me. "Those who cling to worthless idols forfeit the grace that could be theirs." We had to say many goodbyes, prepare many staff recommendations, and tie up loose ends. The morning of the inauguration, we walked out to a lovely tribute from the Naval Enlisted Aides, where they saluted us as we walked between their two lines, forming a path for us to officially depart the VPR for the last time. They gave each of us one of their aprons, engraved with our names and their official coin, which is in the shape of the Residence. It was a moving moment.

The inauguration of a president and vice president is a vivid reminder of how great our nation is. Four years earlier, we had been the ones entering office, and now we were leaving. Mike and I attended the peaceful transition of power, as President Biden and Vice President Harris were sworn in, then headed to our car, where the Secret Service whisked us to Andrews Air Force Base for our last ride aboard what had been Air Force Two. These planes are only officially called Air Force Two if the acting vice president is on board. Charlotte, Audrey, and Dan were waiting. We headed to Indiana, where our friends and family and supporters, some going back to our very first campaign for Congress, were on the tarmac in the cold, waiting to welcome us home.

I felt a peaceful sense of satisfaction, that we had been called over the last twenty years to serve, and we had answered the call to the best of our abilities, and now we were coming home. I thought back to all of the opportunities God had given me, the mantle of leadership He had placed on my shoulders over and over. I thought back through the accomplishments, the struggles, the trials, the achievements, the times I didn't really want to go where He was sending me. Yes, it would have been easier to shrug off the mantle, to give it less than my all. But in the end, I now wanted to know in my heart that when it had been "my turn," with His grace, I had stepped up and accepted the challenge. Everyone has those opportunities at one time or another—perhaps not in the same way that I'd experienced them. But we are all in the position of influence in our own spheres. Hopefully this recollection of the journey where God has taken me will be an encouragement to you, the reader, a motivator of sorts, as you face challenges and opportunities in your life when it's your turn. That is my prayer.

A few weeks before we left the Vice President's Residence, Charlotte gave me a poem she had written while taking a poetry class at Harvard that semester.

I have to admit, I had grown attached to the VPR bees, had learned so much from them along the way, and hoped somehow they would remember me.

"Her Bees Will Stay"

her bees will stay
feed the flowers, keep them going, appreciate the ones planted
*   just for them,*
they have a home here, but the wind decides where they flit,
they promise her they will keep it up,
hunting for the perfect slice
moving toiling sweating
coming home from a long day,
put their feet up and hold hands after dinner by the fire,
picking a television show is always a task
then it's too late and off to bed again,
turn off the lights and know
that tomorrow's work still means something,
even unseen,
they did their best, do their best, now rest;
i love you, goodnight,
ignore those outside,
eyeing the hive

Epilogue

*Wild honeybees create their hives in hollow trees,
openings in rocks, and other spots that scout
bees think will be good for their colony.*

After we officially returned to Indiana and were greeted by our wonderful supporters on the tarmac at Columbus Municipal Airport after the inauguration, we spent a night at Aynes House with Charlotte, and Audrey and Dan. It was a bittersweet moment, knowing we needed to head back to D.C. the next morning for a four- to six-month transition period. Mike would subsequently launch Advancing American Freedom, a policy and advocacy organization. We weren't out of the fight, just out of office.

At that time, we still didn't have a home in Indiana, even though we had spent some time looking a few weeks before. On top of finding a permanent place to live, there were other things we had to do. I needed to finish my school year, the culmination of a thirty-year teaching career, and Mike was creating the foundation. We were renting a house in Northern Virginia and looking daily online for a home in Indiana. In addition to setting up the organization, Mike had many opportunities that began presenting themselves, including speaking engagements and writing his memoir.

The morning I saw our now-home for sale on the internet, I called out to him and said, "I found our home!" He came and looked at the pictures on the internet, we called our Realtor, and she went directly to the home and FaceTimed with us from the house. We got on a plane to Indiana the next morning.

We spent three hours at the home that afternoon, and I could see Mike relax while we spent time on the property. We both knew that God had truly brought us home. He had gone before us once again, searching out a place for us to camp. And not just camp . . . but to put down roots. There's another verse I love that says God will settle the Israelites in their homes. I felt He was doing that for us. The first weekend after we moved into that home, we held a celebration. We hosted a wedding picnic for Audrey and Dan for our Hoosier friends who hadn't been able to travel to Hawaii for their wedding and a Harvard graduation celebration for Charlotte. We went to the Indianapolis 500, which has been a tradition in our family for years, ever since I had first used my paper route money in sixth grade to purchase my first ticket to the "Race." Yes, this was a place we could build memories with our grandkids, have friends over, and celebrate special occasions. This was home.

Since then, there have been many special moments and we know there will be more in the future. Our three children and their wonderful spouses are thriving; we have three beautiful grandbabies, and we have the perspective to truly appreciate what we have.

While we are no longer in office, we have immersed ourselves once again where God is calling us, whether that is helping our kids and their families, visiting refugees crossing the border from

Ukraine into Poland, or spending quality time with veterans and their spouses in marriage retreats with Samaritan's Purse in Alaska. We've served Thanksgiving meals in Florida to those who suffered from Hurricane Ian. We've also made an effort to just be good neighbors and enjoy ice cream socials and barbecues with new friends and old.

I can rest in the fact that when it was my turn, I answered His call. I stepped off that cliff and trusted Him to carry me, to lift me up to where He wanted me to serve. And He did. And he will continue to do so. Just like He will with you, when it's your turn.

After the honey is harvested, the bees do not stop, they do not quit. They start again making more honey, raising more worker bees, and continuing with their purpose.

ACKNOWLEDGMENTS

As I write these acknowledgments, so many names and faces are swirling through my mind . . . people who have been a part of my life over the years and have supported me or helped to shape who I am. However, this book is not a memoir. This book is intended to encourage the reader along their journey as I expound on the ways God used me to help others. And so, while there are so many people near and dear to my heart, those acknowledged here by name are those who have played a specific role in supporting my efforts as a congressional spouse, as first lady of Indiana, and as second lady of the United States. Many of my closest family and friends are hidden here in the pages, just because they are part of who I am, and are not listed specifically. To all of those who have helped shape who I have become, who have given me the strength and fortitude to persevere throughout my life, you know who you are. Thank you from the bottom of my heart. While your names may not appear on these pages, they are written on my heart.

To accomplish as much as I was able during my tenure as first lady of Indiana and second lady of the United States requires an amazing team. A team consisting of my loving and supportive family, good friends, prayer warriors, and dedicated staff.

To David Vigliano, my agent, thank you for your kind shepherding of this idea, and wanting just the right fit for a publisher. To Tom Flannery, you are such a gifted wordsmith and encourager. You knew how to guide me to bring the story out onto the page while keeping my vision.

To my publisher, HarperCollins, thank you for your enthusiasm and excitement. You made me get excited!

To my editor, Hannah Long, thank you for helping me to craft just the right message.

Writing this story was a journey that I had the privilege of taking with my daughter, Charlotte Bond. Her countless hours of typing long-distance while I dictated, her experience as an author, her skill at arranging the story in a succinct manner, and her gentle encouragement made the process a joy and a lovely mother-daughter memory we both will cherish.

Thank you to my friends who lived this journey with me: Karen and Larry Klee; Ruthie McIntosh; Bill and Carol Stephan; Kathy Riley; Jim and Jane Wainwright; Kirsten Phillips; Jamie Broyles.

Thank you to my Indiana First Lady's Charitable Foundation board, Bev Bush, Marilyn Logsdon, Nancy Bush, Debbie Gabe, and Brenda Gerber Vincent, and to Matt Morgan, who helped us navigate legal; to my First Lady's Luncheon committee, Patti Coons, Denise Pence, Sandy Hageman, Jennifer Ping, and Laura Schellinger, and to Annie Grinstead and her team at Positive Energy who made the First Lady's Luncheon so spectacular each year; to my Indiana Governor's Residence Foundation board: Jane Wainwright, Carol Stephan, Nancy Lawton, Phyllis Garrison, Simona Hasten, Janet Hubler, Denise Jackson, the late Vicki Lake, and Shelley Triol; to our very generous Sanibel friends, Reese and Linda Kauffman, and our very generous Vail friends, Bo and Nancy Elder, and our Aspen friends, Toby and Melissa Neugebauer; to all of the many, many supporters in all of the campaigns and the generous donors and vendors and contractors who helped us to be good stewards of the Indiana Governor's Residence and the Vice President's Residence.

Thank you to my extended family: Cyndi Barcio, Marsha and Jim Louzon, Lillian Barcio, Bernie Barcio, Nancy Pence Fritsch, Ed Pence, Basil Fritsch, Gregory and Denise Pence, Edward and Kim Pence, Thomas and Melissa Pence, Judy Pence, Annie Poynter, Mary and Kevin Walsh, all of my nieces and nephews.

To my prayer warriors, Diane Bond, Sue Schwien, Jane Wainwright, Julie Brown, Linda Armstrong, Nancy Bennett, Lynn Brown, thank you for the years of weekly prayer sessions; your prayers made all the difference.

To those who followed my congressional prayer email for twelve years, and those along the way who would greet us, grasp our hands, and say, "We're praying for you."

To so many staff members, thank you. You made me look good. First of all, to my first lady staff, Brenda Gerber Vincent, my chief of staff the first year; Brenda Morrissey, my chief of staff for three years; the late Marilyn Fernandez, deputy chief of staff; Meredith Bullock, personal assistant. My second lady staff, Kristan Nevins, chief of staff the first year; Jana Toner, chief of staff for three years; Kara Brooks, director of communications and also my press helper as first lady (even though she officially worked for the governor); Sara Egeland, policy director; Cynthia Andrade, Residence manager; and Joye Harrison, Estephania Gongorra, Natalie Swan, Emily Lair, Halee Dobbins, Megan Schray, Ericka Morris, Annabel Rutledge, Noelle Spencer, Steve Whitaker, Lauren Hagen, and Jenny Tuggle.

To God, who counted me worthy to serve, thank You for stretching me. Thank You for calling me. Thank You for giving me the courage to step off that cliff.

To my precious family. Thank you for being the constants in this journey. The Bible says, "God places the lonely in families." I am so grateful for my children and their spouses and my grandchildren.

Michael J., you know me so well. Thank you for your calm presence, thank you for sharing all of your check flights with me first, thank you for what you do every day for our country, thank you for your support and your love. Sarah, thank you for your insights always about life, thank you for your amazing strength, thank you for your sense of humor that so often lifts my spirits.

Charlotte, thank you for your gift of words, thank you for your careful crafting of each sentence you put on the page, thank you for asking me to illustrate your first book, now one of many, and thank you for your love. Henry, thank you for your deep faith and sacrifices you have made for our country.

Audrey, thank you for always talking things through with me and helping me find my voice, thank you for your heart and the way you give me such confidence, thank you for your wisdom beyond your years and your love. Dan, thank you for your quick wit and generous spirit, always willing to spend time and energy on others.

Michael, thank you for being my helpmate for thirty-eight years, never relegating me to the shadows, but holding my hand so we both could stand in the sun through this journey.

RESOURCES

1. "About the American Art Therapy Association." American Art Therapy Association. https://arttherapy.org/about/#:~:text=DEFINITION%20OF%20ART%20THERAPY,experience%20within%20a%20psychotherapeutic%20relationship.

2. Brook Brown, Kara. "How Do Bees Prepare for Winter?" *Waxing Kara*, May 2, 2022. https://waxingkara.com/bees-prepare-for-winter/.

3. "Fun Facts." *American Bee Journal*, February 29, 2016. https://americanbeejournal.com/tiposlinks/fun-facts/.

4. Garamone, Jim. "The Story of the Pentagon 9–11 Flag." U.S. Department of Defense, September 11, 2014. https://www.defense.gov/News/News-Stories/Article/Article/603220/.

5. "Honey Bee Facts—50 Things You Never Knew about Honey Bees!" Buzz AboutBees.net, February 16, 2021. https://www.buzzaboutbees.net/honey-bee-facts.html.

6. "Honey Facts." Treasure Valley Bee Rescue. http://www.treasurevalleybeerescue.org/honey-facts/.

7. "How Do Honeybees Make Hives?" Orkin, October 1, 2021. https://www.orkin.com/pests/stinging-pests/bees/honey-bees/how-do-honey-bees-make-hives.

8. "Indiana Bicentennial Celebration 2016." IBC: Legacy Projects. https://www.in.gov/ibc/2351.htm.

9. "Life in a Hive." Bees: A Honey of an Idea. Canada Agriculture and Food Museum, University of Manitoba. https://bees.techno-science.ca/english/bees/life-in-a-hive/guarding.php.

10. M. Amsey. "Honey Bee Facts." Apex Bee Company. https://www.apexbeecompany.com/honey-bee-facts/#:~:text=Honey%20bees%20use%20the%20sun,and%20how%20far%20to%20fly.

11. "Our Story." Veterans Art Project. https://www.vetart.org/our-story.html.

12. Sahe, Dane. "Fun Facts about Bees and Beekeeping." Wild West Honey, July 14, 2019. https://www.wildwesthoney.biz/bee-smarts-b/bee-facts-about-bees-and-beekeeping.

13. "The Warrior Is a Child." Lyrics.com. STANDS4 LLC, 2023. Web. 20 Mar. 2023. <https://www.lyrics.com/lyric/1236408/Twila+Paris/The+Warrior +Is+a+Child>. Written by: TWILA PARIS. Lyrics © Universal Music Publishing Group. Lyrics Licensed & Provided by LyricFind.

14. Thompson, Rosemarie. "How Do Bees Make Honey?" *Sanctuary Gardener*, December 31, 2013. https://sanctuarygardener.wordpress.com/2013/09/06/how -do-bees-make-honey/#:~:text=A%20colony%20of%20bees%20will,make %20one%20pound%20of%20honey.

15. U.S. Naval Observatory. https://www.cnmoc.usff.navy.mil/usno/.

ABOUT THE AUTHOR

KAREN PENCE, former second lady of the United States, is a mother, educator, and watercolor artist. Mrs. Pence dedicated thirty years in the classroom as an elementary school teacher. She became the first lady of Indiana in 2013. In her role as the first lady of Indiana, Mrs. Pence created the Indiana First Lady's Charitable Foundation, a 501(c)3, established with the purpose to encourage and support youth and families of Indiana. The foundation's board awarded over $600,000 in grants to charities throughout Indiana in three years.

As the second lady of the United States, Mrs. Pence was committed to raising awareness and educating the public about the mental health profession of art therapy in the United States and around the world.

In September 2018, Mrs. Pence launched an awareness campaign to elevate and encourage our nation's military spouses. As part of the campaign, Mrs. Pence educated military spouses about the available resources and opportunities to support spouses and their families.

Mrs. Pence has illustrated three children's books written by her daughter, Charlotte Bond, featuring their pet bunny, Marlon Bundo: *A Day in the Life of the Vice President*, *A Day in the Nation's Capital*, and *Marlon Bundo's Best Christmas Ever*.

Mrs. Pence earned a BS and an MS in Elementary Education from Butler University in Indianapolis. She is a Blue Star mom. Mrs. Pence and Vice President Mike Pence have been married since 1985 and are proud parents of their adult children: Michael and his wife, Sarah; Charlotte and her husband, Henry; and Audrey and her husband, Dan. The Pences have three granddaughters: Avery Grace, Etta Rose, and Elena Marie.